KU-566-490

CONTENTS

INTRODUCTION

The aim of this report is to provide up-to-date research findings about the development and education of very able pupils, and so improve communication between researchers and those who make and carry out practical educational decisions. Although it does touch on some theories, the text is primarily concerned with work with the very able which can be assessed on compared results, whether statistically analysed or demonstrable. Because the reported studies reflect different educational systems and outlooks, national contexts are provided along with descriptions of the procedures. Not all of the several hundreds of references from which this information has been drawn can be provided in the confines of this book, so those chosen are the ones which are considered important markers in the field.

It is clear from the evidence that excellence does not emerge without appropriate help. To reach an exceptionally high standard in any area very able children need the means to learn, which includes material to work with, focused challenging tuition and the encouragement to follow their stars.

This research report focuses on the three most frequently asked questions:

- Who are the very able?

- What are the very able like?

- How to educate the very able?

PART ONE:

WHO ARE THE VERY ABLE?

DEFINITIONS: POTENTIAL AND ACHIEVEMENT

The very able are defined here as those who either demonstrate exceptionally high-level performance, whether across a range of endeavours or in a limited field, or those whose potential for excellence has not yet been recognised by either tests or experts. There is a distinction between the recognised gifts of children and those of adolescents and adults. The children's are usually seen in precociousness in comparison with others of the same age, and the adults' in productions based on many years of dedication to the chosen domain.

Aptitudes may range across different areas, such as intellectual, artistic, creative, physical and social, or be limited to one or two. But whatever the potential, it can only develop into exceptionally high achievement in circumstances which are rich in the appropriate material and psychological learning opportunities. Arguments about precise definitions and the identification of such children have been active for nearly a century, and will doubtless continue. However, it is educationally more productive (and more scientific) to look at achievements in terms of the dynamic interaction between individuals and their opportunities for learning throughout life. Children with potential for outstanding performance may need educational provision which is not provided by non-specialist schools.

In this report, the terms 'very able' or 'high ability' are used, as well as that troublesome word 'gifted', with its implications of gifts bestowed intact from on high. The term may be further modified with adjectives: moderately gifted, very gifted, highly gifted, profoundly gifted, seriously gifted, average gifted etc., suggesting the possibility of precise identification along a single spectrum of abilities, usually IQ. It is also claimed, without scientific evidence, that at the highest (or most profound) levels, such children are likely to be warped in personality and emotional development, and so should be treated differently from 'average' gifted children. Human abilities, though, however advanced in childhood, are always relative and inevitably change during life (Arnold & Subotnik, 1994).

Nevertheless, as almost all international researchers use the term gifted it would be verging on the deviant to avoid it. Genius is a description usually saved for adults, referring to the few who have made an innovative and lasting impact on a global scale, typically Albert Einstein, Marie Curie or Pablo Picasso. In the United States, though, it has been applied to small children (e.g. Terman, 1925-1929), although none of the sample of 1,572 actually became adult geniuses (Holahan & Sears, 1995).

Distinguishing high-level potential as distinct from measurable achievement is particularly difficult because the true potential of very able children, who are 'merely' working above average level, is easily missed. Research shows that the very able are not a homogeneous group, whether in terms of learning style, creativity, speed of development, personality or social behaviour. Consequently, there are perhaps 100 definitions of 'giftedness' around, almost all of which refer to children's precocity, either in psychological constructs, such as intelligence and creativity, but more usually in terms of high marks in school subjects (Hany, 1993). In formal school education, for example, social or business talents are rarely considered, and physical and artistic prowess are frequently seen as inborn potential which can be developed to excellence by coaching and practice. To some extent, the way a very able child is defined depends on what is being looked for, whether it is academic excellence for formal education, innovation for business, or solving paper-and-pencil puzzles for an IQ club.

Does giftedness last?

Evidence from follow-up studies shows that high test-scores or marks in school are not a reliable indicator of adult careers, except for those who continue in a similar path, such as teachers and academics (Freeman, 1991; Subotnik *et al*, 1993; Holahan & Sears, 1995). Using children's precocity as the prime identifying feature of high ability is probably responsible for its later apparent loss, often called 'burn out', which is usually due to the others catching up.

The Goertzels' (1978) study of 317 eminent adults found that two-thirds of them were not in any way precocious, and Gardner's (1993, 1997) case-studies of 11 world-changers found that even by the age of 20 only Picasso's future world status was apparent. Schools *are* effective, though: they can change children's perceptions about themselves, with notable effects on their lifelong achievements, to the extent that the earlier the child starts in formal education the more likely that child is to reach a high level of school achievement (Sylva, 1994). But overall, schools appear to have relatively less effect on the fulfilment of gifted potential than that of pupils of more average ability, possibly because they do not, on the whole, focus on the development of the pupils' special gifts (Subotnik *et al* 1993).

The major difficulty with follow-up studies of gifted children is that almost all begin with children chosen by extremely high scores on tests, usually either of IQ or school attainment. This restricts the range of abilities and achievements available for investigation, and so affects the reliability of any predictions. However, a unique study in California began with 130 one-year-olds of unknown potential, the only criterion being that they were healthy (Gottfried *et al*, 1994). Various measures of intellectual, physical and social development were made regularly until they were 9 years old. Those with an IQ of 130 or more on the Wechsler Intelligence test were designated gifted and compared with the others. The researchers concluded that giftedness is a developmental phenomenon, which can rise and fall over time: 'late bloomers' do exist and can be missed in a single testing. A rich educational environment is essential to develop intrinsic motivation, curiosity and love of learning, which Renzulli (1995) calls 'task commitment'.

Predicting adult excellence

In a survey of the research on prediction, Trost (1993) calculated that less than half of "what makes excellence" can be accounted for by measurements and observations in childhood. He found intelligence and other cognitive factors to be the most reliable indicators, but, given a high level of aptitude, the key to success lies in the individual's dedication.

Follow-up studies of gifted children began with Lewis Terman (1925-29) who by 1928 had selected 856 boy and 672 girl "geniuses", almost all from California, eventually producing more than 4,000 variables. There were, however, considerable flaws of procedure, e.g. "no private, parochial (religious) or Chinese schools" (Holahan & Sears, 1995, p. 11). The subjects, aged between 2 and 22, were mostly children of white university staff, sometimes of Terman's colleagues. The sample was collected over a period of 7 years. The children were first selected by teachers then tested, those with IQ 135 plus being taken into the sample. The general population was used for comparison. But even by 1928 a quarter of this sample of 'Termites' (as they came to be known) had vanished from the study and were simply replaced, and leavers continued to be replaced for years. Terman's "geniuses" were considerably above-average in every way, including height and leadership qualities, but then they did have above-average nourishment and education. The latest review of the 'Termites' in their seventies and eighties shows that they have not been noticeably more successful in adulthood than if they had been randomly selected from the same social and economic backgrounds regardless of their IQ scores (Holahan & Sears, 1995). Perhaps because of their relatively privileged upbringing, they had an exceptionally high level of self-confidence and the creativity to make plans and stick to them: they have lived longer and more healthily, and are still more actively involved than the general population.

In spite of the doubts about the research design, the Terman results are in accord with more scientific longitudinal work by Schaie (1996), who found that intellectual and perceptual abilities remain high for individuals who are active and open-minded, but in particular, those who feel satisfied with their life's accomplishment in mid-life are at a considerable advantage as they age. The Munich Longitudinal Study of Giftedness began in 1985 (Perleth & Heller, 1994). It has a sample of 26,000 children, identified on a wide variety of intellectual, personality and achievement tests, although personal interactions with the children have only recently been introduced. The team devised 30 identification scales, which disclosed a significant number of underachievers, who were characteristically found to be anxious, easily distracted and to have poor self-esteem.

In a review of 14 American and German follow-up studies of varying design and loss of subjects over time, Arnold and Subotnik (1994) pointed to several important factors in the conditions for the development of talent. They suggest an "inextricable link" between the identification of potential and timing due to age-related stages of development, so that accuracy in predicting achievement increases with the age of the sample studied. The child's own interests appear to be an excellent and often neglected indicator of adult attainment (Renzulli, 1995: Hany, 1996; Milgram & Hong, 1997). Accordingly, for the greatest reliability, information should be collected at different points in an individual's life, most reliably within specific subject areas in which the child shows promise and interest.

A 15-year follow-up of 82 'valedictorians' (the highest grade earners in high school) from 32 schools across Illinois showed that even such exceptional grades were not good long-term predictors of later high achievement (Arnold, 1995). The research was thorough, with each individual being given five or six interviews after leaving school. They had enjoyed all aspects of school, which they found to be a supportive social environment, and had used it efficiently to prepare for their future lives. Their major academic advantage was in their determination to better themselves. Neither boys nor girls felt themselves to be outstandingly clever nor had they been labelled as such; in fact, during their college years, the women continually lowered their estimates of their intelligence. None of this sample made outstanding progress in their careers (particularly the women), and at 26 years old many were disillusioned.

The long-term benefits of early special provision for the gifted are still far from certain. In spite of an initial higher measured achievement, the advantage tends to disappear over a few years (White, 1992). But these discouraging results have mostly been based on the old-style pattern of IQ-identified gifted children being given the only provision available at that time. Much knowledge has been accumulating and the future of education for the very able is undergoing major changes in outlook, which may well bring improved results for more children.

WAYS OF IDENTIFYING THE VERY ABLE

Each method of identifying the very able distinguishes a somewhat different group of children, with possibly different consequences for their self-concepts and education. For example, because a high IQ score is to some extent a measure of school-type achievement (see below) it is good at picking up children who will continue to do well at school, but it is not very helpful in identifying sporting prowess, which is decided by experts. The problem with any form of selection for special provision is that if promotion of the skills and talents needed by society is limited to an elite, however skilfully that elite is selected, there will inevitably be individuals whose potential contributions remain undeveloped or who must find other routes to fulfilment. And, because it is not possible to predict the kinds of talents that will be needed in the future, there has to be a wide variety of skills and outlooks available in any society. Research is presented here on the four most frequent methods of identification: 1 Intelligence; 2 Teacher recommendation; 3 Parent recommendation; and 4 Peer nomination.

1 Intelligence

Very high intelligence, as measured by IQ tests, is by far the most popular criterion for defining children as very able or gifted. However, after more than a century of use, this procedure is still highly contentious. Just one problem is that IQ testing is strongly influenced by belief systems which include social and moral values. An example is in the Stanford-Binet Intelligence Scale in the question "What's the thing to do if another boy/girl hits you without meaning to do it?". The correct response must involve forgiveness.

The concept of intelligence is changing

A wider and generally accepted view of intelligence is that it is an individual way of organising and using knowledge, which is dependent on the social and physical environment. Consequently, conventional methods of measurement, notably the IQ test reflecting the old ideas of relatively fixed capacities, are being replaced by measures which aim to distinguish the many components of intelligence, so that they can be presented as profiles of ability, such as in the British Ability Scales. Other standardised tests are available in specific areas, such as for musical or science aptitudes.

There is also growing influence of the Theory of Multiple Intelligences conceived by Howard Gardner at Harvard (Gardner, 1983). He argues that human abilities are best considered as at least seven distinct intelligences, only two of which, linguistic and logical-mathematical, fall within the usual definitions of intelligence. The other five, spatial (chess, painting etc), musical (playing or appreciation), bodily-kinaesthetic (sports and gymnastics), interpersonal (social skills) and intrapersonal (self-awareness), have usually been regarded as talents. Gardner has recently added to this list with naturalist intelligence (knowledge of the living world), spiritual intelligence (cosmic issues) and existential intelligence (ultimate issues). However, the evidence for their distinctiveness has not been replicated by other researchers, who usually find that these 'intelligences' overlap. Schools have now been set up in the USA where the children are taught via these intelligences, and in Britain the University of the First Age in Birmingham, which helps underachieving children, is basing its enrichment provision on these ideas (UFA, 1996).

In contradiction, Gagné (1995) of Montreal has proposed four aptitude domains (intellectual, creative, socio-affective and physical) and four talent fields (academic, technical, artistic and interpersonal). Their development, he suggests, depends on the learning context, normally the school, which should recognise the child's own efforts.

Sternberg (1993; 1997), at Yale, warns that it is important to be aware of what is culturally valued and what is not. This influences the way one shapes one's activities in everyday life, and must be part of any assessment of intelligence. His Triarchic Theory of Intelligence is concerned with applications of processes, which he says can be used in schools. For example, linguistic aptitude could be channelled into the child's natural preferences - analytic (as in criticism), creative (as in poetry) or practical (making advertising copy). For him, high ability is the development of one's natural aptitudes to an exceptional level. Renzulli (1995) emphasises task commitment, creativity and innate ability as indications of giftedness. Recent work (e.g. Subotnik *et al*, 1993) has also shown that high ability may take many different forms; it may appear in quite unexpected situations and at different points during a lifetime.

There is considerable evidence for biological differences between the highly able and other children. This implies that there is a limit to how far teaching can bring on a pupil. The IQ scores from studies of more than four hundred sets of identical and non-identical twins separated at birth were investigated in later life (Plomin *et al*, 1994: Bouchard, 1997). This work has discovered considerable genetic influence on intelligence, at about 70% the strongest correlation found for any psychological characteristic. Such studies have also highlighted environmental influences, notably that the younger the child the more potent the environment. But no specific gene for giftedness has yet been discovered. Lykken *et al* (1992) concluded from their separated twin research that specific talent appears to be an 'emergenic' trait, one which depends on a particular configuration of genes, so finely balanced that any small difference will result in distinct changes of behaviour. Indeed, we know that constant stimulation of the brain and its responses can change its fine structure and function for life, as shown by the use of visual techniques for helping dyslexics (Bakker, 1990). The sleep rhythms of intellectually gifted children appear to be different from the average; they have more REM (rapid eye movement) sleep (Grubar, 1985; Dujardin *et al*, 1990). Some psychologists, such as Eysenck (1995), have claimed that intelligence (the ability to learn) can be measured by speed of reaction. This would be a very helpful guide to teachers, if the experimental results were not so unreliable.

IQ tests

Intelligence is usually measured by IQ tests. High ability or giftedness is then determined by a score which is above a chosen cut-off point, usually at around the top 2-5%. But it is important to know which test has been used. The two most popular tests, the Stanford-Binet and the Wechsler Intelligence Scales, measure IQ somewhat differently. The Stanford-Binet is verbally biased while the Wechsler is mathematically biased, and the upper limits of each differ by 20 IQ points, which makes comparisons between scores at their upper ends difficult. But they are not even an adequate measure of intellectual giftedness because of the 'ceiling effect', whereby highest measures of the tests are too low to distinguish satisfactorily between the top few per cent. What is more, some children get every item right and could obviously score more highly were the test to accommodate them. Some psychologists calculate additional IQ points above the test's ceiling, even to beyond IQ 200 (e.g. Gross, 1993, Silverman, 1993), though there is no scientific basis for this. Much current research and theory, though, is indicating that intelligence, however it is defined and measured, is only part of the complex dynamics of exceptionally high-level performance, which must include such matters as self-esteem, support, motivation - and opportunity.

A very close positive relationship was found when children's IQ scores were compared with their rated home educational provision (Freeman, 1991). The higher the children's (Stamford-Binet) IQ scores, especially over IQ130, the better the quality of their educational support, measured in terms of reported verbal interactions and activities with parents, number of books and musical instruments in the home etc. Because IQ tests are decidedly influenced by what the child has learned, they are to some extent measures of current achievement based on age norms. The vocabulary aspect, for example, is dependent on having heard those words.

IQ tests can neither identify the processes of learning and thinking nor predict creativity (Cropley, 1995; Urban, 1995), and because they only measure a narrow band of intellectual behaviour they cannot predict other aspects of life, such as what career a person is likely to follow or how individuals will cope in social situations. In fact, drive and energy have often been found to be relatively *more* predictive of life success than high IQ in children (e.g. Albert, 1992; Holahan and Sears, 1995; Subotnik *et al*, 1993; Schaie, 1996). There are other kinds of intelligence tests, however, such as the more culture-fair Raven's Matrices, which do not contain specific learned material, such as words, and instead use pattern matching. Teachers can use these tests with groups, which are useful as a general guide to reasoning ability. They do not result in an IQ score, but offer a percentile (where the score is described as a percentage of all values lower than or equal to it). It must be noted, though, that they have an even lower 'ceiling' than the IQ tests, the upper limit being the 95th percentile, and so they cannot differentiate very well between the top 5% of children.

Nevertheless, in spite of the evidence pointing out the debits of the IQ score as a measure of an individual's all-round ability, it has been proved many times to be a valid and reliable measure of potential for achievement **in school,** the purpose for which it was designed. When the IQ score is taken into account along with the understanding of the test used and as a part of an assessment it provides a useful and reliable tool for identifying academic ability.

Can gifted performance be learned?

Studies of successful people brought Howe (1990) to the conclusion that "in the right circumstances almost anyone can" ... acquire exceptional skills (p.62). He argues that self-direction, self-confidence, a sense of commitment and persistence can effectively produce gifted performance. Indeed, without a cello, tuition and a family to back him Yo Yo Ma could not have become a great cellist, whatever his talent; but then, if one were to give other children the same provision, would they also turn out to be virtuosi?

Attempts to teach gifts have been carried out in American laboratory studies which for some years have been analysing the specific skills of expertise (Ericsson & Lehman, 1996). However, even in those strictly controlled conditions the trainees differed in the level of expertise they could reach, and the researchers found (as have many others) that motivation and practice (as any teacher knows) make a vast difference to results. The researchers concluded that the most important variable in gaining expertise is sufficient ability to gain a foothold in the learning process, and then to put in thousands of hours of learning and practice. This was also found in Holland (Elshout, 1995) in a study of expertise in children solving physics problems. They were selected for intelligence (High and Low) and their expertise in physics (Advanced v Novice), resulting in four groups (n = 28). The difference between the Highs and the Lows was much larger in the Novice group than in the Advanced group. Experienced Lows outperformed Highs of less experience, indicating that experience compensated for lower intelligence.

Even for high-level artistic performance it has been said that "formal effortful practice is a principle determinant of musical achievement" (Sloboda *et al*, 1996, p. 287). In an earlier contradictory statement, though, when reporting work in Britain with school-age talented musicians in Manchester, he found that "the best students had done *less* formal practice in their early years than had the average students" (Sloboda, 1993, p.110). Rather, he found that the best students had received more praise then the others, and their parents had made them feel 'special'.

Cultural and family attitudes have a considerable effect on high-level achievement. For example, Berry (1990) found highly significant geographical and religious differences between Nobel prize-winners. In proportion to their numbers, Jews were heavily over-represented, in certain subject areas 50 times more. Zuckerman (1987) suggested that as 75% of Jewish Laureates came from lower socio-economic backgrounds, it could not have been social advantage which produced that excellence, but rather, in line with other research, the cultural influence of the family's drive for success. Indeed, in their late adulthood, the most successful of the Terman sample were distinguishable neither by IQ nor by earlier school achievement but by family background, notably the aim for success (Holahan & Sears, 1995). In many Pacific Rim countries, as well as Russia, measured intelligence is largely ignored and success is attributed to sheer effort, hence the growth of out-of-school crammers. His investigations led Flynn (1991) in the US to conclude that the culture of hard work is probably responsible for so many Asian-American (usually meaning Pacific Rim) youngsters' greater school and work success than their higher IQ classmates. In fact, Hess & Azuma's (1991) in-depth research showed that American children needed much more help and praise than Japanese children in their motivation to learn.

2 Teacher recommendation

Naturally, teachers' judgements of their pupils' abilities affect their expectations and treatment of them. This can be seen in the organisation of learning groups and selection for examinations, which will in turn affect the pupils' attitudes to education. When pupils move to more challenging work, both teacher and pupil expectations are increased (Good, 1996). We do not know, though, how any teacher's personal conceptions or stereotypes of giftedness affect his or her actual teaching.

There can be wide variation between teacher judgements and objective measures. Individually, teachers' attitudes towards the very able vary greatly; some feel resentment while others overestimate their all-round abilities, as was found in a Finnish-British survey (Ojanen & Freeman, 1994). But teachers have been found to judge the highly able consistently, in that they will continue to pick the same kind of children (Hany, 1993). In England, Bennett *et al* (1984, p.215), found that 40% of potentially high achievers had been underestimated by their teachers, and Nebesnuik (from Eyre 1997, p. 17) "showed a significant discrepancy between the assessment of able pupils by their primary teachers and subsequently by year 7 teachers" [pupils aged about 11-12]: the primary teachers often chose children as able by their ways of working rather then their cognitive ability. Using IQ as his criterion of giftedness, Tempest (1974) in Southport, UK, found that out of 72 six year-olds identified by their teachers as gifted, only 24 had IQs of 127 or above and seven had IQs of under 110. But two children with reading ages six years in advance were not nominated as gifted. He concluded that teacher recommendation alone was not reliable.

Hany (1997), in Germany, investigated how 58 secondary school teachers judged giftedness, using a rating scale of 60 suggested traits. The teachers were seen to be biased in their judgements in certain respects. They did not fully consider the basis of comparisons or non-obvious characteristics, in that they would choose pupils who were most like their expectations. Creativity was not often seen as an aspect of giftedness, and emotionally the gifted were often expected to be playful, arrogant, uncontrolled and even disturbed. The teachers often kept a mental image of a gifted pupil who would have exceptionally good logical reasoning, quick comprehension and intellectual curiosity in combination with good school grades. Individual gifted pupils were often vividly remembered by teachers, who would use those characteristics to identify others. But when teachers were offered guidance by the researchers on how to identify the gifted in their own subjects they found it very helpful, particularly because of their day-to-day knowledge of the pupils.

How teachers perceive and thus identify the gifted has been seen to vary considerably between different cultures. The estimations of more than 400 secondary teachers in Germany and 400 in the USA were compared with 159 in Indonesia. The German teachers estimated 3.5% of children as gifted, the Americans 6.4% and the Indonesians 17.4% (Dahme, 1996). Even within one country, the USA, percentages of the child population identified as gifted vary between 5% and 10% across the states, although most now have legislation and financial support for 'gifted education' (OERI, 1993). It is to be expected that the definitions and special facilities provided by educational authorities would have some effect on teachers' choices.

In an investigation into mathematics teachers' attitudes towards able pupils in 500 English comprehensive schools, the researchers presented them with suggested lists of the characteristics of mathematically able children (Chyriwsky & Kennard, 1997). The teachers generally agreed with these, but also expressed concern that such pupils were both educationally underchallenged and frequently deterred by peer-group pressure. The teachers often felt hindered by constraints on time and material resources in teaching bright pupils, and that any available extra provision was targeted towards the least able.

Research in Oxford used experimental checklists for teachers in 11 comprehensives to identify the top 10% of third-year pupils (year 9) in their own areas of expertise: physics, mathematics, English and French (Denton & Postlethwaite, 1985). However, these check-lists were up to 22 items long, which teachers found off-putting, and this resulted in a low response rate. Further, the research did not make use of objective criteria, such as standardised test scores or the pupils' eventual O-level results. Instead, only the teacher-set classroom tests were used, which, as they were marked by the same teachers, could be self-fulfilling. The best items for accurate teacher prediction of test marks made use of the more obvious characteristics, such as verbal ability for English tests, and mathematics for mathematics tests. In French and physics, clear errors of teacher judgement were found, more noticeable at the start of the school year than at the end when the pupils were better known to the teachers. Both this Oxford and the German studies (Hany, 1995) were in accord that teachers mostly judged high potential by general rather than specific abilities. Both, though, found that high abilities were subject-specific, and suggested that this focus was the most likely to produce the most accurate predictions.

In Russia, teachers' opinions, intelligence tests and a creativity test were used to select 73 children aged 7-8 as gifted (Sheblanova, 1996). Both this group and a random control group of 76 children were tested yearly for three years and their results compared. Large intellectual differences were found between the groups, although only 54-60% of teachers' ratings had predicted these. The teachers were good at selecting the high-level achievers, but had difficulty in identifying high-level intellectual and creative ability. Interestingly, although there were no differences in scores between the sexes on intelligence or creativity, the Russian teachers still considered the girls to be more gifted, whereas in Israel, using check-lists, teachers chose two boys for each girl (Shahal, 1995).

A multiple criteria identification procedure for primary school selection of the very able was devised in Jordan (Subhi, 1997). The research involved 25 schools with 4,583 third-graders (8-9 year-olds) of whom 217 (4.74%) were identified in a wide trawl using standardised tests for intelligence, creativity, achievement, mathematical skills and task commitment (all translated into Arabic), as well as peer, self, teacher and parent nomination. Teachers' nominations were found to have missed 50 pupils with IQs above the cut-off point of IQ 130. The highest IQ children were the least likely to nominate themselves. But in the peer-nominations more boys than girls were nominated, even when the girls had equally high IQs. This is the case not only in the Middle East, but in Midwestern USA (Peterson & Margolin, 1997). There, teachers from two middle schools were asked to recommend children for a gifted programme. The teachers appeared to treat "giftedness" as if it were an absolute and universally agreed set of characteristics, and were sure of their decisions. But Latino children, and those from other minority groups, were found to have been passed over.

The above research on teacher nomination of very able pupils is pertinent to the Revised National Curriculum in Britain, which allows some flexibility in deciding at what depth to teach, although the possibility of extension tests to assess more intense teaching has been abandoned for the stated reason that: "the cost of extension papers was not justified by their use … most [simply] drew on the programmes of study for the next key stage." (DfEE/SCAA, p.11). Consequently, as Standard Attainment Tasks (British SATs are also known as 'end-of-key-stage-tests' and used for the 4 key age-related stages) only measure the three core subjects of English, maths and science: "The Secretary of State proposes to place *sole reliance on teacher assessment* [my italics] for the award of levels to exceptionally able pupils" (DfEE 1996, p.4). However, teachers are not being given any help in assessing their most able pupils - with all the potential problems of misjudgement outlined above.

Research-based methods by which teachers can recognise very able pupils

- Use the outcomes of particular tasks set for pupils, rather than simply test scores or work-books. In smaller groups, recognition can be helped by subject-orientated discussion.

- Children's abilities change over time; some may develop later than expected while others may show a sudden drop in achievement. Because human memory is unreliable and easily affected by current impressions, teachers should keep careful records in checklist format.

- Focus on particular aptitudes, rather than apparent general intelligence or positive attitudes to school work.

- Personal interaction between teacher and pupil is important to find non-obvious talents.

- A second observer from time to time is a help.

- Check that choices are not biased by social class, ethnicity, gender or handicap etc.

- Watch for bias – make sure that all pupils have access to the facilities available.

- Recognise pupil efforts and techniques which attempt to overcome handicaps.

- Use as many assessment procedures as possible.

- Watch out for motivation and interests as clues to potential.

- Consider more pupils than are immediately obvious. Positively seek variety – look through the range of subject areas for pupils with diverse talents.

- Take more than one opinion, perhaps a group decision; but remember that groups can be dominated by strong characters and that a majority decision may not always be right.

- Lively activity outside school and little interest inside school can indicate gifted underachievers.

- Consult the pupils themselves.

Checklists

Checklists of the supposed characteristics of highly able children vary considerably, and some of the items can be confusing. Some, rather than being specific to aptitudes, may be socio-cultural. For example, a child asking a lot of questions can either be seen as gifted or as attention-seeking, or perhaps lives in a home where questioning is encouraged rather than one where children are encouraged to work things out for themselves.

One list may ask the teacher to look out for dedicated seriousness, while another suggests a keen sense of humour: although in a rare survey of experimental work, humour has not been found to have any relationship with creativity or intelligence (Galloway, 1994). While one list may point to a tendency to perfectionism (and thus procrastination), another will describe the highly intelligent as speedy decision-makers. Some see introversion as typical features of the high IQ child, although there is no reliable evidence of any personality features being associated with IQ.

American lists, in particular, sometimes suggest a higher level of morality and leadership in the gifted, for both of which there is little evidence when social class, home support etcetera are recognised. Indeed, in Finland, Merenheimo (1991) showed that "self-confidence and moral development of students aged 13-16 was firmly anchored to the influences of microcultures" (p.116). Although there is a positive statistical relationship between scores in tests of IQ and tests on morality (such as Kohlberg's Moral Development), a survey of international research by Adreani & Pagnin (1993) could not find any recognisable relationship between IQ and *actual* behaviour. In another survey of research into moral giftedness, the American, Rothman (1992) pointed out that "IQ explains but little in the development of moral reasoning" (p.330). He suggested that the higher scores of high-IQ children on moral reasoning tests result from their enhanced social interaction with adults. It is as though the intellectually gifted know what they should answer on the tests, but may or may not choose to abide by their answers.

Checklists (even official ones) can mislead. For example, one British LEA publishes this list (given here in full) of the characteristics of the able child, which mostly asks the teacher to look for signs of emotional distress, which is quite contrary to the evidence (see page 27).

- "Prefers friendship with older pupils or adults.

- Excessively self-critical.

- Unable to make good relations with peer groups and teachers.

- Emotionally unstable.

- Low self-esteem, withdrawn and sometimes aggressive."

(NIAS, 1994, p. 15, quoting George, 1992)

Another misleading characteristic often presented in checklists is poor-quality sleep, which has no scientific support. In fact, Terman reported that the most gifted in his sample slept longer and more soundly than the others. When Browder in Germany (in Perleth, 1993) managed to compare the sleep of children whose giftedness was unknown to their parents with non-gifted children, there were no differences in pattern or quality. Freeman (1991) found that children's length of sleep, as reported by parents, was directly related to their age, and not to intelligence or achievement. However, the children who were seen as gifted by their parents were described by them as sleeping badly and having more emotional problems than children - of equal measured ability- whose parents did not see them as gifted. Much of the stereotype of gifted children with sleep problems appears to come from parents.

The best that can be said of checklists is that they may stimulate teachers to think about the identification of the very able: the worst is that potentially high-achieving children who do not fit with the opinions of those who devise the lists will be missed. The most reliable research-based criteria which distinguish the highly able and could reasonably be used in a checklist are listed here (From Shore in Montgomery, 1996; Freeman1991).

A research-based checklist for very able pupils

- Memory and knowledge – excellent memory and use of information.

- Self-regulation – they know how they learn best and can monitor their learning.

- Speed of thought – they may spend longer on planning but then reach decisions more speedily.

- Dealing with problems – they add to the information, spot what is irrelevant and get to the essentials more quickly.

- Flexibility – although their thinking is usually more organised than other children's, they can see and adopt alternative solutions to learning and problem-solving.

- Preference for complexity – they tend to make games and tasks more complex to increase interest.

- They have an exceptional ability to concentrate at will and for long periods of time from a very early age.

- Early symbolic activity – they may speak, read and write very early.

3 Parent recommendation

The strangely stable ratio of two boys for every girl in identifying the highly able occurs internationally when parents (and usually teachers) recommend children as gifted without tests. This was the proportion in an American study by Johnson and Lewman (1990) of parents' selection of four to six year-olds as gifted. In China, in a 15-year follow-up study, in which parents made the judgement of giftedness first, which was then confirmed by the teachers, there were 69.5% boys and 30.5% girls (Zha, 1995b). Given the supposed differences in the Chinese attitudes, in which girls are seen as inferior, remarkably similar proportions appeared in Freeman's UK study (1991) where parents made the first recommendation – 64.3% boys and 35.7% girls. The reason appeared to be that the boys had more behaviour problems as well as being more demanding in general. This also fitted better with the stereotyped image parents had of the gifted child.

In the Freeman study, 82% of the parents who had sought help from the National Association for Gifted Children (UK) either reported emotional problems or were expecting them. Typically, the child showed over-activity, clumsiness, tantrums, excessive demands, poor sleep and had few friends of any age. However, the comparison children in the study - of identical high ability - who did not exhibit problem behaviour, were much less likely to be seen as stereotypically gifted (simply outstanding at what they did) and their parents did not join the association. This is yet more evidence that without outside comparisons the study of any voluntary association's membership is inevitably biased, which is equally true for a study of Mensa members.

Freeman also found that about 10% of the children presented (though untested) by parents as gifted were only of average ability on IQ tests, and had achieved accordingly at school. This perceived 'failure' was then sometimes blamed by parents on the school, or indeed as teacher discrimination against the child. However, most of the children presented as gifted were indeed so, as measured by IQ and specific tests of talent, even when the teachers were dismissive of the child's exceptional potential. But parents and teachers were in accord that these association children did have emotional problems, significantly much more (p< 0.1) than the non-association children of equal ability.

4 Peer nomination

In Montreal, Gagné (1995) asked 4,400 pupils, mostly in mixed-ability classes, to choose and rank the four classmates they thought were the best in a particular category - intellectual, creative, socio-affective and physical. Boys and girls were ranked very differently: boys were most frequently chosen for masculine attributes such as physical or mechanical-technical abilities or business, whereas girls were chosen for language, social strengths and art. The researcher's conclusion was that, despite the originally socially desired gender pressures that produced these achievements, these were the actual talents the children displayed, and so the peer judgements were correct. No comparisons were made of these results with any objective tests of abilities, nor of the children's self-estimates. The likelihood of classmates discovering hidden potential seems slight. Subhi (1997) found that in Jordan peers did not nominate any pupils differently to those identified by teachers.

Brakes on identification

Cultural values may inhibit the achievements of bright youngsters at school. These may be quite specific, such as directing girls into nursing rather than medicine. But they can be more subtle, such as the effect of expectations which vary considerably across cultures. If children do not fit those stereotypes they are less likely to be recognised as potentially highly able. Currently, the most common Western stereotype of a gifted child is of a weedy lad: he (for he is usually male) is bespectacled, lonely, and much given to solitary reading. He is, in fact, a juvenile 'egg-head', at times referred to by his schoolmates and maybe his teachers as 'the little professor'.

Very able children who do not speak the language of the test-makers or who think in different ways are also less likely to be recognised as having high potential. In an overview of 20 research-based international papers on the gifted disadvantaged across all five continents, Wallace and Adams (1993) concluded that it is not only culture which can cut such children out of recognition and special provision, but poverty. There is, they wrote starkly, "the equation, in reality, of wealth with giftedness, special educational provision and giftedness" (p.446).

Shore and his colleagues (1991) reanalysed international research on the gifted disadvantaged and listed research-based indications of ways to overcome such handicaps to fulfilment as learning difficulties (e.g. dyslexia) and physical disabilities. These guidelines also apply to children with emotional problems, who have lost self-confidence and who prefer to hide their gifts rather than stand out from the crowd. Passow (1993) pointed out that disadvantaged groups are often handicapped by the test situation itself owing to lack of experience with tests, which produces inhibiting test anxiety, along with low motivation and poor expectations of success. Child-initiated learning, including high-quality peer interaction, has been found to encourage a sense of self-efficacy or empowerment, especially in deprived bright children, compared with teacher-initiated learning, which aims more specifically at a 'product', usually in high examination marks (Ari & Rich, 1992). The list below is a composite:

Identifying disadvantaged highly able children

- Use tests which are less dependent on words (e.g. the Raven's Matrices).

- Use a variety of identification procedures, tuned where possible to specific cultural rather than national norms.

- Look for a broad range and wide variety of high-ability children, and do not label one group as *the* gifted.

- Recognise that discovering and nurturing talent are not the same thing.

- Use the best results from multiple criteria, and provide multiple opportunities for discovery, not multiple hurdles.

- Recognise performance outside the school environment.

- Recognise multilingual capacity.

- Recognise the ability to be competent in situations which have different expectations of the children.

- Include peer, self and parent nomination for high potential.

- Encourage children to initiate their own projects and learning.

- Take the children's facilities for learning into account.

THE BEST WAY TO IDENTIFY THE VERY ABLE

Identification by provision

Identification by provision implies offering a challenging education for the highly able. Like any other pupils they need this *consistently*. Researchers are in agreement that the very able cannot make progress without the means to learn. Consequently, a notable educational move is taking place, away from the relatively static labelling of specific children as gifted towards a more flexible developmental approach which recognises the learning context. This new outlook is nicely summed up by the Americans Treffinger & Feldhusen (1996), who, after very many years of school-based research in this area, now describe the blanket term gifted as "indefensible".

This movement away from static towards dynamic assessments of giftedness was partly initiated in the 1920s by the work of Vygotsky (in Wertsch, 1990) on the Zone of Proximal Development (ZPD), this being distinct from the Actual Developmental Level (ADL) (also promoted by Reuven Feuerstein in Israel: see Feuerstein & Tannenbaum, 1993). The idea is that with specific provision (scaffolding) and mediation (adult guidance, especially through language) children can learn at a far greater speed than otherwise. For young children, Vygotsky pointed to guided play as a rich context for the development of the ZPD in exploring new knowledge and ideas. Kanevsky (1994), investigated the ZPD of 89 4-8 year-olds, asking each child to learn, transfer and generalise a specific problem. She found that "The benefits of high IQ were not as consistent as of chronological age" (p.163). Some high-IQ children made up their own challenges when they were bored, but their learning could deteriorate when they were offered the same curriculum as their age-peers.

The Dynamic Theory Of Giftedness (DTG) is based on Vygotsky's developmental concepts of "plus- and minus-giftedness" (Vygotsky, 1983). This uses the dynamic paradigm that either giftedness or defectiveness are possible outcomes when a child is faced with barriers to development. There are many examples of successful overcoming, as when Alicia Markova, the prima ballerina, took up ballet because of physical problems. Failure to overcome such barriers, though, can lead to a child hiding behind the weakness, which then becomes reinforced.

In an important six-year experimental study in Moscow, Babaeva (1996, and 1998 in press) investigated how to overcome such barriers in 31 children aged 6-7, identified as non-gifted by teachers and conventional tests. She compared their progress on a specially devised system of education with two control groups, identified gifted children in 'normal' gifted education and non-gifted children in regular education. The main goal was to help children develop effective means of overcoming psychological barriers to promote their desire for self-development. By the end of the first year, the average IQ in the class had increased by 10 points, especially verbal IQ, as had creativity, and there were fewer emotional problems. After six years, according to the report, measures of the experimental group's abilities were equal to those of the identified gifted children, and considerably surpassed those of the non-gifted control children.

Such an interactive approach, considering aptitude and provision together, places less emphasis on school marks, and seeks instead to find and provide for potential strengths and talents of all kinds. A clear indication of the need for this was shown in the British Sports Council's research on the Training of Young Athletes (Rowley, 1995). A three-year longitudinal study involving 453 athletes aged 8-16 years examined ways in which the children began participating in sport – who had identified the potential, and why the youngsters started intensive training. It was apparent that the identification of high-level sporting talent was heavily dependent on provision for both tuition and practice, which often depended on parents, as well as on the motivation of the children themselves. Thus, sports clubs and coaches could only play a secondary role in identifying talent, as they could only select already high achievers who had been encouraged and provided for by their parents.

To accommodate this new, flexible approach in finding the potentially very able, special educational techniques are needed, which are different from the conventional route (at least in the USA) of an IQ test followed by a gifted programme which is often simply more school-type teaching. Treffinger and Feldhusen (1996) suggest that there should be considerable involvement by the pupils in identifying themselves as they come to understand their own potential and decide their own goals. Nor does this mean a one-off self-selection; it should be continuous over the school years, resulting in a flexible open-ended talent profile which is regularly added to by all those involved, especially the pupil.

All the evidence indicates that specific provision within subject areas is by far the most effective in promoting excellence, rather than general enrichment without identified goals. This might be, for example, a journalism class for sharp writers or photography for the visually talented. It is helpful to observe children in rich and varied educational settings; perhaps a dancer in a serious dance class, or future programmers with access to good-quality computers. Without high-level learning opportunities it is hardly possible for highest-level potential to flower. The focus is particularly important because unevenness in gifts is more likely than being superb at everything. Consequently, it makes more sense to look out for specific talent in addition to an IQ test.

Able youngsters' leisure activities have been found to be a reliable predictor of future high achievement in that area (e.g. Feuerstein & Tannenbaum, 1993; Renzulli, 1995; Hany, 1996). Although such choice is largely self-directed, showing task commitment, intellectual abilities, persistence and other personal attributes, it also depends on provision. Eighteen years after secondary school, 48 of the original 159 subjects of a high school in Tel Aviv, Israel, were surveyed for their occupational accomplishments and outstanding career achievements, and with few exceptions were seen to have focused on a single domain of endeavour (Milgram & Hong, 1993). A third of the sample had continued to work seriously in their childhood leisure areas with relatively much higher attainment than their school-fellows whose careers were unrelated to their interests. It was concluded that serious adolescent leisure activities were highly indicative of future successful careers and that this form of self-identification should be encouraged and provided for.

Identification by provision in practice

Recent work is beginning to reflect the outcomes from this wider and more child-directed approach. At the Szold Institute in Jerusalem, Zorman (1997) is working on experimental education, termed Eureka, which takes special education for the highly able away from the medical model of 'diagnose and treat', and uses instead a dynamic approach looking at the outcomes of exposing children to opportunity in the visual arts and sciences. It is based on a seven-year follow-up of 60 talented pupils. The model is now implemented in 56 schools and includes all the country's religions. The assessment process uses teacher ratings of pupils' behaviour, professional evaluation of portfolios and task performance. The research also uses self-report questionnaires both inside and outside school, including the children's social behaviour. Voluntary out-of-school enrichment activities are available, from which children's talents are also assessed. Hence the assessment net is flung widely. Although the pupils are generally above average, it has been found that the most important predictor of their success is their high motivation within the chosen subject area. There are also indications that pupils' reading comprehension has been improved, and that their interests have been extended beyond the visual arts and sciences.

Another Israeli example of self-selection through provision is at The Technological Centre for the Galilee, dedicated to the study of ecology (Brumbaugh *et al*, 1994)). The centre works in concert with the local comprehensive school, from which teenage boys and girls have been invited over the past 18 years to work on their own projects under supervision. They are not selected in any way. The centre has the specific aim of developing scientific thinking, using projects such as the effects of magnesium on plants, or cultivating wild mushrooms, or the effects of hormones on fish reproduction. At the laboratory, youngsters design and conduct work on original problems for which there are no existing answers nor (often) methods, then continue to work with the data back at school. The teenager has to prepare and write a research proposal, which is discussed with the laboratory supervisor, submitted to the Ministry of Education for approval, then he or she can begin, either alone or in a group. Each youngster has to be able to work on a computer, and eventually to provide a bound dissertation. The Centre displays the youngsters' work, which is sometimes of Master's degree standard. The cost is low and largely supported by the state.

The Children's Palaces in China practise a very different and highly successful means of identification by provision with primary school children, which again relies on the children's own motivation and interest for its success. (Academic reference exists in Chinese.) Each 'palace' is simply a large house with rooms crammed with activities. Whole schools of mixed-ability children come at one time and are let loose. Some run right through into the playground while others head for the calligraphy, puppet theatre, stationary bicycles, science labs, music rooms etc. The children are not tested for aptitude, but many are stimulated by the novelty of what they discover there to want to learn more. The rules are simple. Those who want to take their chosen subject further must make a contract to come for a specified number of lessons. If they do not attend them all (without good reason) they cannot continue. Some come for years and reach breathtaking standards in their chosen field. Normal teachers are paid extra for this work, which they say they greatly enjoy.

Freeman's Sports Approach

Excellence in some abilities is more acceptable than in others in all cultures. In Britain, for example, local education authorities normally encourage keen, talented footballers to benefit from extra tuition outside school hours, provide them with equipment, arrange transport for them to meet and engage with others at roughly the same level as themselves and pay for it all. Although there is some provision around for other subjects, notably music, and there are mathematics contests and extra-curricular activities, such as art classes in museums, the idea of opening up the school labs for a Saturday morning practice in chemistry is rare, if it exists at all. It is not difficult or expensive to find out what interests and motivates pupils, via questionnaires, interest tests or simply by asking them. Furthermore, the facilities are already largely in place to provide excellent support for abilities other than football.

Freeman (1995) has proposed that, given the opportunity, and with some guidance, the talented (and motivated) should be able to select themselves to work at any subject at a more advanced and broader level. She terms this the 'Sports Approach'. In the same way as those who are talented and motivated can select themselves for extra tuition and practice in sports, they could opt for extra foreign languages or physics. This would mean, of course, that such facilities must be available to all, as sport is, rather than only to those pre-selected by tests, experts, family provision or money to pay for extras. This is neither an expensive route, nor does it risk emotional distress to the children by removing them from the company of their friends. It makes use of research-based understanding of the very able, notably the benefit of focusing on a defined area of the pupil's interest, as well as providing each one with the facilities they need to learn with and make progress.

But to practice identification by provision, the evidence is that teachers will need specific training in differentiated teaching methods, in addition to a variety of techniques for bringing out high-level potential. For example, there would have to be some training in collecting information for a portfolio, or at least some unification of approaches within a school or authority, as well as some form of recognition of what provision the pupils had access to. This could be done by a simple rating scale so that children who were excelling within their context would be seen to be doing so and not penalised because they had fewer opportunities than others. It is a very difficult concept to put into practice, though, as American positive action has shown. The answer lies in allowing wider and easier access to all education, particularly higher education, perhaps as in European universities which accept all applicants with basic qualifications. Suggestions as to how this might be practised are offered here:

The Sports Approach: identification by provision

- Identification should be process-based and continuous.
- Identification should be by multiple criteria, including provision for learning and outcome.
- Indicators should be validated for each course of action and provision.
- The pupil's abilities should be presented as a profile rather than a single figure.
- Increasingly sharper criteria should be employed at subsequent learning stages.
- Recognition should be given to attitudes possibly affected by outside influences such as culture and gender.
- The pupils must be involved in educational decision-making, notably in areas of their own interest.

Educators who might act on the conclusions from research into high ability should be aware of the particular problems in this field, and from what stance this report has been written. Scientific research described here is considered to be the objective assembly of data using a recognised methodology, followed by statistical analysis, interpretation and conclusions. The collection and reporting of statistics is not scientific research *per se*; rather it is part of the provision of material for the research. Nor are personal impressions scientific research, however frequently experienced, well recorded or intensely felt. For example, a summer school for highly able children may give them a great deal of pleasure and companionship as well as increase their knowledge, which the organisers perceive as highly satisfactory; but only comparative experimental research could tell us whether a particular kind of provision is more appropriate for the very able than another, or whether all children might well benefit from those activities.

Researchers' attitudes to the very able vary widely. Some favour the case-study approach because they say a gifted child is unique and so cannot be compared, whereas to others the gifted are normal children with exceptional aptitudes. The case-study approach can be vividly illustrative, but in order to be most effective and rigorous it has to be set in a wider social context to justify generalisations. For instance, if one high-IQ child refuses to go to school, is this really typical of a frustrated future Einstein in a mixed-ability class, or could it be because of subtle messages from home that the child is 'too clever' (and by implication too sensitive) to fit in?

How typical is the sample group?

A variety of methods are used to select highly able children for studies. Some samples are made up of children who are already highly achieving, and because of that have been selected for vacation courses or special 'gifted' education. How much of their subsequent improvement can then be said to be due to the special treatment, and how much to the fact that the best predictor of future success is present success? There should be some comparison of the selected group with children of different abilities and educational experiences.

This lack of comparison was notable in a study by Benjamin Bloom (1985) of 120 young Americans who had reached "world-class levels" of accomplishment. He concluded that certain family influences were vital in the promotion of talents, particularly encouragement combined with discipline and good teaching. This seems reasonable, but we do not know the effect of similar parenting behaviour on other children, even on the siblings in those families, because no such comparisons were made. Nor was any reference made to possibly inherited aptitudes; all the credit for talented achievement was presented as entirely environmental. The study was also retrospective, relying on memories of early years, and as most of the interviews were done by telephone, there was no independent assessment of the children's social or physical environments. We do know that many parents work extremely hard at training their children for great accomplishments - without success - while others, such as Leonard Bernstein's father who sold the piano because his son practised too much, actually discourage their talented children.

Many often-referenced studies use tiny and so perhaps unrepresentative samples, such as that of six American boy "prodigies" who were followed up for 10 years (Feldman with Goldsmith, 1986). They did not continue their advantage into exceptional adult achievement, a feature of 'hot-housed' children. Nevertheless, a complex theory of giftedness emerged from that study, including the idea of "trace elements" – a combination of unrecognised chance events which are essential for gifted performance – some might call it luck. In Australia, Gross (1993) used the contentious IQ of 200 to select just three "profoundly gifted" young children. They were described as exhibiting the 'typical' symptoms of emotional disturbance, such as school-refusal, and were without any friends because to them being with normal children was akin to interacting "solely with children who are profoundly intellectually handicapped" (p.475).

Looking back at the lives of eminent adults (e.g. Goertzel *et al*, 1978; Radford, 1990; Albert, 1992) also presents problems of interpretation, such as unreliability of memory, the perception of early experiences in terms of later achievements, and the different outlooks of those times which brought those people to eminence. In truth, although we can never identify and measure the full context of anyone's life, even in the present, there are certain basic scientific research concerns which should be in place before expensive and life-changing action is taken, based on the conclusions from findings.

Improvements needed in researching the very able

- Clearly defined theoretical bases and statements of goals for extra provision.

- Comparisons of outcomes from different forms of provision e.g. enrichment or acceleration.

- Generally acceptable scientific standard of methodology and case-study reports.

- Cross-cultural and cross-social comparisons to test concepts of universality.

- Comparisons of experimental interventions in and out of places of education.

- Investigation into high-level learning and thinking.

- The effects of labelling children as very able.

PART TWO

WHAT ARE THE VERY ABLE LIKE?

HIGH-LEVEL THINKING AND LEARNING

Scientific-type thinking is not restricted to science. It is thinking which can cope with the relationship of theory to knowledge, and which provides the flexibility to revise what you 'know' in the face of fresh evidence. It is the root of the development of the skills needed to justify assertions. The thinking of more successful learners, even as children, has been found to be closer to that of experts, in that they make more reference to what they already know, rather than only to the information presented in given problems. This was seen in Canadian work by Shore *et al* (1992), who audio-taped and analysed young children's thinking-aloud comments. Although some researchers have concluded that the learning procedures of the gifted are more mature (Luthar *et al*, 1992), others find them to be different in style (Kanevsky, 1992). The value of knowledge, though, is not to be underestimated: it is vital to outstanding performance. Individuals who know a great deal about a specific area are seen to achieve at a higher level than those who do not (Elshout, 1995).

Emotions help or hamper learning at all levels. German research on gifted young children has found that fear can inhibit the development of curiosity, an important motivator in learning, thinking and creative endeavour (Lehwald, 1990). Boekaerts' (1991) overview of international research on the learning of gifted young children found that those who achieve most highly are not only very curious but have a hunger to learn, often along with a strong urge to control. Canadian research with young children has also found an extra quality of playfulness in the learning of highly able little children (Kanevsky, 1992). Investigating the current work of creative scientists in California and later that of living "classical" composers, although some of this work was retrospective, Simonton (1988; 1991; 1994) could demonstrate that above a certain high level, personal characteristics such as independence contributed more than intellect to reaching the highest levels because of the great demands of effort and time needed. Perhaps for that reason, a four-year follow-up investigation of talented American teenagers by Csikszentmihalyi *et al* (1993) found that in learning to tackle difficult tasks, the stronger the social support the more developed the youngster's skills, though schools were found to be much less effective in this than parents.

Self-regulation in learning

Self-regulation implies autonomous learning, being able to prepare and supervise one's own knowledge acquisition, to provide one's own feedback and to keep oneself concentrated and motivated. The equation is relatively straightforward: the more able an individual the more self-regulation will be needed for high achievement; the less able an individual the more teacher regulation is needed (Span, 1995). Indeed, applied research into how children learn science brought Adey (1991) to the conclusion that "the children's ability to think about the nature of their own thinking was a critical contributor to success". Conversely, teachers who are too directive can diminish their pupils' learning autonomy. Although 'spoon-feeding' can produce extremely high examination results, these are not always followed by equally impressive life successes (e.g. Kaufman, 1992; Arnold, 1995).

After 20 years' work in this area, Merenheimo (1991) in Finland concluded that "gifted pupils have an analytic strategy of perceiving information. The less gifted use either atomistic or serialistic strategies" (p.115). He believes this results from learned habits upheld by social experiences. Indeed, for the more average pupil, when teacher regulation is missing they often fall back on simple trial and error and rote-memorising, which can become a difficult habit to change. But Wertsch (1990) found that guided conversations with young children, helping them to understand the way knowledge and arguments could be practised, resulted in a measurable shift from teacher to self-regulation.

If, as the evidence indicates, the intellectually gifted think and learn differently from others, then it is important to teach them appropriately. Overviewing research on the thinking process of highly able children, Shore and Kanevsky (1993) put the teacher's problem succinctly: "If they merely think more quickly, then we need only teach more quickly. If they merely make fewer errors then we can shorten the practice."(p. 142). But this is not entirely the case, they say; adjustments have to be made in methods of learning and teaching to take account of thinking differences. There is now ample scientific evidence which shows that in order to learn by themselves the very able need some guidance from their teachers (Paris & Byrne, 1989). To be at their most effective, pupils can be helped to identify their own ways of learning which include strategies of planning, monitoring, evaluation, and choice of what to learn. They should also be helped to be aware of their attitudes to the area to be learned, such as curiosity, persistence and confidence.

When teachers help pupils to reflect on their own learning and thinking activities they are increasing their pupils' self-regulation. For a young child, it may be just the simple question: what have you learned today? which helps them to recognise what they are doing. Given that a fundamental goal of education is the transition of the control of learning from teachers to pupils, improving pupils' learning to learn (metacognition) should be a major outcome of the school experience, especially for the highly able.

To help teachers in schools, Nisbet (1990) distinguished these five methods:

Promoting self-regulation in learning

- *Talking aloud*. The teacher talks aloud while working through a problem so that the pupil can see the working.

- *Cognitive apprenticeship*. In this the teacher demonstrates the processes that experts use to handle complex tasks, guiding the pupil via experiences.

- *Discussion.* This must involve analysis of the processes of argument.

- *Co-operative learning.* The pupils explain their reasoning to each other. Co-operative teaching-learning interactions in the classroom are ideal for helping pupils take the leap to higher levels of understanding.

- *Socratic questioning.* In this, the teacher uses careful questioning to force pupils to explain their thought processes and explain their arguments. The questioning is not used to teach new knowledge, but to help pupils to know and use what they already have.

VERY ABLE GIRLS AND BOYS ARE DIFFERENT

The effects of being a boy or girl are different for the highly able than for those of more average ability (Freeman, 1996a). Many studies have shown gender to be the strongest single influence on high-level achievement, possibly owing in part to the 'glass ceiling', the invisible social barrier that prevents high-ability females from fulfilling their true career potential. German evidence has shown that intellectually gifted girls appear to be more like gifted boys than girls of average ability (Stapf, 1990). Emotionally, though, in America they have been found to be more depressed than equally able boys, often underestimating their abilities because of conflicts between success and 'femininity' (Luthar *et al*, 1992). Golombok and Fivush (1994) write that: "Careful statistical analyses across hundreds of studies have demonstrated that gender differences in ability in math and language are so small as to be virtually non-existent for all practical purposes" (p.177). They conclude that the measurable sex differences in aptitude are due to "a complex interaction between small biological differences and larger gender differences in socialisation experiences" (p.176).

There are currently changes in school achievement in Britain, showing that at school girls are achieving higher national examination grades than boys in *all* subjects. Although some other countries are moving in this direction, notably Australia, the situation in Britain appears to be unique. Investigating this, the Equal Opportunities Commission considered that better school inspection was partly the reason for the relative improvement in girls' achievements (Arnot *et al*, 1996). Women now make up 51% of university graduates (about the same in the USA and 61% in Russia), but in all countries men reach very much higher positions in their careers (e.g. of all British full professors and high court judges, women make up less than 5%).

An experimental intervention programme in Indiana gave girls 'directed enrichment', after which they were able to reach much higher levels in a variety of talent areas (Moon *et al*, 1994). Investigating mathematically precocious American youth in the USA, Benbow & Lubinski (1993) found that although gifted girls did significantly better on standardised tests in mental arithmetic and computation, they were much less successful with higher-level problem-solving, and much less frequently studied mathematics at a higher level. While recognising the effects of cultural influences, they reached the conclusion that there is a genetic mathematical bias in favour of boys, although the British figures refute this.

When girls start school in America they are identified in equal proportions to boys for gifted programmes, but as they get older there is a striking loss in the proportion of girls selected for gifted education (Winner, 1996). Although girls make up half the gifted population in kindergarten, this proportion shrinks to less than 30% at junior high school, and even less at high school, and so on. Asian American girls (usually meaning those from Pacific Rim countries), though, are an exception; they score more highly on Scholastic Aptitude Tests (American SATs are used to decide college entrance) than non-Asian girls. It has been suggested that they are born with a different brain structure (in Benbow, 1988), a conclusion which is clearly untrue for girls in other cultures.

Gender expectations

Taking a long-term look at giftedness in mathematics in the USA, Jacobs & Weisz (1994) found that parents held somewhat fixed and conventional gender expectations. This influenced the girls' self-esteem more than their actual performance, and inhibited their ambitions. In agreement, teachers questioned in 722 schools and 136 colleges in England and Wales reported that the main reason for low take-up in advanced mathematics and science was the perceived difficulty of the subject – more true for girls than boys – and for girls there was the added lack of women teachers as role models in these subjects (Sharp *et al*, 1996). According to Smithers (1997), physics A level is the only area in which girls' grades may be beginning to decline again because the earlier exam is a more general measure of "scientific literacy", whereas A levels are a high-level selection device for university which picks out different ambitions and character traits. However, the published examination results appear to contradict him.

An international review of research on gender differences in the highly able in mathematics and natural sciences failed to find any reliable evidence that girls are inherently less able than boys in these subjects (Heller 1996). So, because they have similar abilities, girls and boys can act as experimental controls for each other to gauge the power of social effects, probably best seen in career outcomes. Heller pointed out, for example, that even on present tests of spatial abilities at which boys do better, we could expect only twice as many male engineering graduates as females, whereas there are 30 times as many. This effect was found to be more pronounced among the gifted, girls being more influenced by social pressures than boys, e.g. by the 'unfemininity' of subjects such as physics, as well as having much less practice and fewer role-models. Most importantly, the often-noted 'learned helplessness' of girls (a feeling that events and outcomes are beyond their control) was considered to be the result of 'wrong' attributions, so that girls often think their success is due to luck rather than their own ability. Thus, Heller states, believing that they are not good at maths, but simply lucky to have done well that time, girls adjust their behaviour to fit their belief (attribution) and 'confirm' it by doing less well as time goes by.

Children's feelings about what they are able to achieve start early. Young children do not understand ability in the same way as they will begin to at about age 11, in that they start by expecting effort to lead to results (Heyman & Dweck, 1996). They learn as they grow up, maybe falsely, that they are not able to achieve high-level results, and so stop trying. Differences in motivation to learn in young children may also be more to do with their ideas of goodness and badness than with specific ideas of intellectual competence. Increasing motivation to learn, then, implies taking the blame away from personal deficiencies, such as perceived low ability over which children have no control, and putting it on lack of effort or appropriate learning strategies over which they *do* have control. Bennett *et al* (1984) emphasised the importance of teacher feedback which enables a pupil to learn from mistakes, rather than, as sometimes happens, giving different feedback to those for whom teachers have high or low aspirations.

Mentoring and counselling to improve self-esteem have been found to be effective in promoting a more realistic acceptance by gifted girls of their abilities (Arnold & Subotnik, 1994; Freeman 1998). German researchers (Heller, 1996) designed a focused and "largely successful" experimental programme of 're-attribution' to help girls recognise and accept their real talents. For this they used personal experience and positive feedback with 19 boys and 23 girls in six one-hour sessions, then compared their achievements with a group who had only attended the school course. Results indicated that re-attribution should be started soon after the bases of the learning had been laid down; another opportune time was at the move from primary to secondary school — prevention, they say, being better than cure. The team stressed that for teachers to really help underachieving gifted girls (or perhaps British boys) they should have special training to use these re-attribution techniques in the classroom situation. One especially effective technique they used was verbal encouragement to increase motivation, e.g. as follows:

Increasing self-esteem for higher achievement

Successful performance

- Emphasise the student's abilities or talents – "The topic suits you".

- Give consistency information – "You have done that right again".

- Give consensus information, and thus stress success – "Most people have difficulties with this problem, but you did it".

Unsuccessful performance

- Attribute it to insufficient effort – "If you read that again it will soon become clear to you".

- Take the edge off failure by providing consensus information – "Most students have difficulties with that".

- Give distinctiveness information – "The other topic suits you better, doesn't it".

There is no reliable scientific evidence to show that exceptionally high ability *per se* is associated with emotional problems, or that an inadequate education results in delinquent or disturbed behaviour. On the contrary, an American meta-analysis pointed to *low* intelligence and attention problems as being associated with delinquency (Maguin & Loeber, 1996). Investigators who describe the gifted as having emotional problems have usually taken their data from clinical settings and case-studies, where the population is self-selecting and no comparisons are ever made with other equally able children (e.g. Silverman, 1993; Gross, 1993) or voluntary gifted children's associations (see above).

However, an American researcher has written: "Like other children, the problems gifted students bring to counselling usually arise from family relationships." (Robinson, 1996, p. 130). When types and degrees of behavioural problems were compared for gifted and non-gifted elementary school children in the USA, there were no significant differences (Cornell *et al*, 1994); similarly, using self-reporting techniques comparing adolescent gifted and non-gifted children, "the gifted students show better adjustment" (Nail & Evans, 1997, p18). It could even be said that the gifted have to be emotionally *stronger* to achieve so exceptionally.

In fact, some studies of the gifted have indeed found them to be emotionally stronger than others, with higher productivity, higher motivation and drive, and lower levels of anxiety. An Israeli study (Kener, 1993, in Zorman, 1996) found that gifted junior-school boys and girls showed significantly higher self-esteem when compared with those of average ability from similar backgrounds. In Italy, a sample of 300 high school pupils were given tests and open-ended questionnaires, although the follow-up only managed to trace 63 of them 8 years later (Boncori, 1996). There were three sub-samples, 'highly gifted' (the top 10% of the general population), 'less gifted' and 'average'. The 'highly gifted' not only had far greater academic success than the other two groups, but also right through university enjoyed better social integration, wider interests, less materialism and more satisfaction.

Specific pressures

High-achieving learners and labelled 'gifted' children are sometimes susceptible to extra pressure from teachers and parents to be continually successful in examinations, possibly at the expense of more challenging intellectual, artistic and emotionally satisfying activities (Freeman, 1997). What is more, no individual can perform at a high level all the time, not least because these children's abilities may develop at different and extreme rates, which can bring difficulties of co-ordination (Terassier, 1985: Silverman, 1993). For example, children who are advanced in verbal ability are not, on average, more advanced in motor skills (Robinson, 1996). Additionally, the highly able may suffer from false stereotyping along a spectrum which ranges from expecting them to be emotionally handicapped to expecting them to be perfect in every respect. Fear of failure and feelings of failure and of disappointing others' expectations are likely to develop, with possibly negative emotional consequences for life.

Social life: The particular pressures which the very able may experience usually stem from others' reactions and expectations of them. For example, although the gifted may be expected to be too clever to enjoy normal relationships with ordinary people, in most findings, higher IQ youngsters have *better* all-round social relationships (e.g. van Leishout, 1995; Boncori, 1996). There is some evidence, though, that under special stresses, such as the certain expectation of top-level examination results, highly-achieving adolescents can become depressed and even prone to suicide (Farrell, 1989; Yewchuk & Jobagy, 1991). Other researchers have pointed to the tendency to perfectionism in the gifted (Stedtnitz, 1995; Robinson, 1996). But we cannot be sure about the causes, or whether this kind of obsessionality is found more among the gifted than other children. Certainly the gifted can suffer from adults who mistake the abilities for the child.

A problem which each talented pupil in a mixed-ability class has to solve is socialising with less able classmates while being intellectually at a higher level, and thus different from them. This calls for exceptional maturity and social skills, since a high level of individuality needs to be shown at some times and conformity to social norms at others. American work by Webb (1993), though, has found that gifted children can sometimes make social problems for themselves: "They often repeatedly and intensely attempt to organise people and things, and in their search for consistency, emphasise 'rules' which they attempt to apply to others. Often they invent games and then try to organise their playmates. Almost regardless of the settings, tensions are likely to arise between the gifted children and their peers." (p.529).

Reports from a 15-year Chinese study of 115 extremely high-IQ children (Zha, 1995b) showed the strong influence of family provision on both achievement and emotional development. The children were first identified by parents (two boys to every girl) and then validated as gifted by a psychologist. Every year parents were given a questionnaire and interviewed several times. The parents-to-be had taken their future responsibilities very seriously by studying parenthood. As the toddlers were learning to speak the parents often taught them to read, and some children even mastered writing at the same time. By the age of three many children could recognise 2,000 Chinese characters, and at four many could not only read well, but also write compositions and poems. However, these 'hot-housed' children were found to be lacking in easy social relationships, and the parents had to be given some more lessons in how to help their children to have some social life.

Popularity: Researching the emotional adjustment of the very able via one-to-one interviews in Germany, Rost and Czeschlik (1994) compared the responses of 50 high-IQ with 50 average-IQ primary school children, and concluded that the former were the better adjusted. Later, working with mixed-ability primary school children, they found that those with high-IQs were the most popular (Czeschlik & Rost, 1995). Brody and Benbow (1986) used American Scholastic Achievement Tests to select mathematically and verbally high-scoring 13-year-olds. Questionnaires about their lives and feelings were mailed to them (response 78%). Although a less able comparison group were only included two years later, it was concluded that the high scorers saw themselves as less popular although more in control of their lives; but as there was no actual contact with the youngsters it was difficult to tell why this was so.

The effect of being labelled: Possibly there is cultural difference in the way children react to being labelled as highly able or gifted. In Croatia, Kolesaric and Koren (1992) experimented with the effects of publicly labelling the top 10% of 11-year-old pupils from 14 schools as gifted, based on four tests of cognitive ability. They were then compared with non-labelled mixed-ability control children, none of the sample being in a special programme. The total sample of 1,215 pupils was examined before and after two years, as were their parents and 300 of their teachers. The selected pupils felt much more frequently than their teachers and parents that the label 'gifted' carried some danger to their developing personalities, and also disagreed with the adults' preference for separate schools. Yet for American youngsters who were in pre-college gifted programmes, their self-esteem was found to be highest when attention was focused on their gifts but lowest when focused on personal relationships (Colangelo & Assouline, 1995). In Israel, too, most of the children in a national survey of special classes for the gifted felt that the label increased their self-confidence (Shahal, 1995).

Research, unique in its in-depth approach, was carried out in Britain over 14 years (Freeman, 1991). This was a comparative follow-up study of carefully matched triads of children, initially aged 5-14. The target group of 70 children, identified by their parents as gifted, were compared with a second group of 70 who were unlabelled - but of equal measured ability - and with a third group of 70 randomly selected children. All were interviewed and tested in their homes across the country, as well as their families and teachers in the schools being questioned. The children were also given a wide variety of tests and their environmental circumstances rated. It was found that those who had been labelled 'gifted' (whose parents had joined the National Association for Gifted Children) had significantly (p< 1.0) more behaviour problems than those of equal ability who were not so labelled. However, the possession of an IQ within the top 2% was not found to be related to emotional problems or social relationships, which were instead associated with other difficulties in the child's life. In fact, the brightest appeared to be exceptionally empathetic. The most practical finding was that at all levels of intelligence (70 IQ-170 IQ) the children's school achievements were directly related to accessibility of facilities for learning, as well as to parental involvement and example.

Ten years later, using the same home interview methods, the labelled young people had often remained the least happy (as measured by rating scales), for which their gifts were sometimes blamed. Labelling appeared to have had the effect of putting pressure on children to live up to it in high achievements, notably in the case of those who had been wrongly labelled and could not fulfil their parents' ambitions. As a result of having highly able children, parents can themselves have emotional problems, whether through feeling inadequate or trying to gain social advantage from living vicariously through their child. Whatever problems already exist in the family, these can be intensified when there is an unusual child present (Freeman, 1993).

Too many talents: Although some youngsters have specific gifts and thus can see their career route quite clearly, there are others who seem to have the potential to do almost anything to a high level. The problems of being able to do a great number of things extremely well arise when vocational choices have to be made, and skilled attention is needed to help young people make the best decisions in that situation (Milgram, 1991; Deslisle, 1992).

For the multi-talented, vocational problems can be more severe than for other pupils. For example, by the age of 17, one highly talented boy in the Freeman sample had acquired degree-level music qualifications, but he also had four A grades in A-level sciences. His dilemma was whether to study music or medicine. After great anguish, he decided to take the science option but found little in common with his fellow medical students. As a hospital doctor he grieved so much for his music that he eventually gave up medicine. Having lost his years of music practice, however, he became a musicians' agent rather than a performer. Specialised vocational guidance for these children should start early, possibly even in primary school. It is distressing and wasteful for all-round highly able young people to change their post-school course, as well as being an extravagant form of vocational guidance.

PART THREE:

HOW TO EDUCATE THE VERY ABLE?

MIXED-ABILITY CLASSROOMS

Ideally, in mixed-ability teaching, the pupils should be following the same theme to different depths, yet many teachers have a natural tendency to pitch the level of their lessons to the middle range of ability. A bright child, waiting for the class to catch up with what he or she already knows, may have to kill hours each and every day. In reality, however, there is probably very little true mixed-ability classroom teaching in Britain today: in 1994 less than 1% of schools used it in all subjects until the age of 16, exceptions usually being art, music or physical education (Benn & Chitty, 1996).

can lead to misbehaviour boredom.

The normal classroom is a fairly structured place, providing activities for which the teacher attempts to harness pupil compliance to improve knowledge and basic skills. But both the uniqueness and the potential enrichment the gifted can bring to a class can be put at risk by conformity. These pupils are often less comfortable than others where there is a rigid teaching structure and limited pupil involvement (Freeman, 1991).

As a result of pressure to excel at school, Sternberg and Lubart (1995) found that the high-IQ highly-achieving pupil often had considerable problems in producing original insightful ideas. More than 200 teenagers in the Yale summer programme were divided via tests for Sternberg's Triarchic Theory of Intelligence into 'high analytics', 'high creatives' and 'high practicals'. Each of these groups was compared with a balanced-gifted group (equally high in all three areas) and a balanced above-average control group. All the young people took a very challenging college-level psychology course, at the close of which they were assessed for basic recall, analysis, creative use and practical use of the new information. The 'high analytics', those who had often been identified as gifted by IQ, did worst of all the groups on the creativity tests. The authors concluded that these pupils had rarely been asked to make a creative effort, but had learned to conform to expectations of being good scholars by using memory to gain high grades. However, investigations into American prize-winners in the arts and sciences showed that a very high intelligence was not always essential for outstanding results – sheer memory was much more useful (Walberg 1995). It seems that whereas memory can be gainfully employed in creative work, it can also be abused for high-level school achievement.

Boredom

A child with a curious and speedy mind can suffer from boredom in an undifferentiated classroom. In America, Feldhusen and Kroll (1991) questioned primary school children about their attitudes to school. The questionnaire responses of 227 gifted children (identified by IQ) were compared with those of a random control group of 226. Although the gifted had normally begun school with positive attitudes, they more frequently complained of boredom, often because of the lack of appropriate challenge. In a similar American survey, 871 academically gifted pupils (identified by IQ and school marks) at each level of education were asked whether they found challenge in their lessons (Gallagher *et al* 1997). They replied that this only happened in mathematics and special gifted classes. But the researchers also cited evidence (p.132) of the absence of differentiated teaching in the American classroom.

Boredom for any child can become a demoralising and maladaptive habit leading to disenchantment with learning. To relieve this unpleasant experience, youngsters may escape into daydreams or deliberately provoke disturbance (Freeman, 1992). Or, when constantly faced with tasks which are too easy, they may make challenges of their own, like testing the rules (Kanevsky, 1994). They may also make mistakes, either because they are not paying sufficient attention, or just to relieve the tedium. A major problem for those who find learning easy is that they may not learn the discipline of study, getting by on what they remember from lessons, for which they will pay a price when they encounter more advanced work.

Another manoeuvre for coping with boredom is the *Three-times Problem*, which Freeman (1991) identified via self-reports. To avoid the boredom of listening to teacher's repetitions, pupils who absorb the information the first time develop a technique of mentally switching-off for the second and the third, then switching on again for the next new point involving considerable mental skill in several psychological areas. However, until this technique is running smoothly, they may miss parts of the lessons, so that teachers may underestimate their abilities. It is understandably confusing because the child seems so bright and yet is apparently not learning. As with all habits, this one tends to persist, especially if it starts early; some of the highly intelligent youngsters in the Freeman sample did not listen carefully to what other people were saying, often, they claimed, being distracted by higher thoughts.

Unfulfilled talent – underachievement

Because of their speed and style of learning, school experiences for highly able pupils are often different from those of other children. In an attempt to make friends and blend with the others in a mixed-ability class, such youngsters may try to hide their exceptionality. Butler-Por (1993), overviewing and evaluating 20 years of special classes for the gifted in Israeli normal schools, found that when teacher expectations were not high, underachievement in the potentially talented was hidden in a just-above-average school performance. She also found that the overriding reason for underachievement was lack of provision for learning. Emerick (1992) identified six alleviating factors:

Reversing the school performance of gifted underachievers

- Encouraging out of school interests.

- Working with parents.

- Co-ordinating goals associated with academic achievement.

- Improving classroom instruction and curriculum.

- Advising the teacher.

- Counselling leading to personal changes in pupil.

Emotional problems or inadequate provision of learning materials can lead to underachievement in any child, which can be exacerbated by mismatches between styles of instruction and learning. West (1991) examined the lives of ten famous visual thinkers, including Einstein, Edison and Churchill, all of whom had 'underachieved' at school. He presented developmental neurological research showing an association between visual talent and verbal difficulty, and concluded that the visually talented can encounter particular learning problems in a normal classroom where teaching is linear (one fact following another in a specified order). Although he does not indicate how such children can overcome these difficulties, he does provide guidelines for their recognition by teachers.

Some indications of learning problems of talented visual thinkers

- Poorly presented work and poor sense of time – possibly over-compensated by excessive orderliness.

- Excessive daydreaming.

- Difficulties with arithmetic – though not geometry, statistics or higher-level mathematics.

- Difficulties with speech – hesitation, delayed development.

- Sometimes poor physical co-ordination.

- Ineptness or lack of tact – but sometimes exceptional powers of social awareness.

- Difficulties in memorising assigned information by rote e.g. multiplication tables – but superb memory for interest areas.

- Difficulty in learning foreign languages, especially in the classroom – but sometimes an exceptional ability with their own language.

- May be overactive, inattentive and 'in their own world'.

LIVERPOOL JOHN MOORES UNIVERSITY
LEARNING SERVICES

Having surveyed the work of many American researchers, Deslisle (1992), in accord with Butler-Por (1993), concluded that all underachievement is a learned behaviour which is always tied to individual self-concept, therefore each case must be judged independently. However, Deslisle does make a useful distinction, between underachievers and non-producers whose school marks may be the same.

Underachievers – are likely to have emotional problems, with poor self-esteem. They find it extremely difficult to make changes to their behaviour on their own and can benefit from counselling help.

Non-producers – are psychologically strong and confident of their capabilities. They are choosing not to comply and are probably successful in their own way, such as in a street-gang, or perhaps are biding their time until they leave school and can choose how to achieve in a non-academic domain, such as in business.

The following indications of underachievement are drawn from various sources (e.g. Treffinger and Feldhusen, 1996, Feuerstein & Tannebaum, 1993, Renzulli, 1995, Hany, 1996).

Some signs of underachievement in the potentially very able child

- Bored and restless
- Fluent orally but poor in written work
- Friendly with older children and adults
- Excessively self-critical, anxious and may feel rejected by family
- Hostile towards authority
- Quick thinking
- Does not know how to learn academically
- Aspirations too low for aptitudes
- Does not set own goals but relies on teacher for decisions
- Does not think ahead
- Poor performance in tests, but asks creative searching questions
- Thinks in abstract terms
- Often enjoys playing with language
- High-level work has deteriorated over time

Some suggestions for helping underachievers

- Affirm worth by praise for even small things

- Daily review of progress

- Involve the pupil in decisions about own education, e.g. setting own learning goals and so increasing motivation to learn

- Make the material relevant to the child's own interests

- Have pupil mark own work before offering it to the teacher

- Tutoring of younger pupils in underachiever's areas of strength

- Mentoring in area of pupil's interests

- Accept pupil without emotional strings

Grouping the highly able for teaching

Differentiation in mixed-ability teaching is often helped by grouping by ability or by a more fluid (e.g. vertical) approach based on mutual interest. An example of the latter is in musical instrument playing, where a group, e.g. of school brass players of varied ages and abilities, can meet to form a band - such interest often being an excellent indicator of talent (Renzulli, 1995: Hany, 1996). British mathematics teachers have been found to strongly prefer setting over streaming, which is in line with the benefits of the subject-specific approach, since streaming means categorising children by their overall ability, while setting relies on independent assessments of ability for each subject (Chyriwsky & Kennard, 1997).

At the National Research Center on the Gifted and Talented in Connecticut, the effects of co-operative learning were compared for mixed-ability and gifted-only groups, with 786 11 year-olds drawn from 42 classrooms (Kenny *et al*, 1995). The results showed that the gifted did not experience any adverse emotional effects from learning with the non-gifted. Quite the reverse; they were seen as more friendly, better leaders and experienced an increase in social self-esteem. The gifted learned about as much as expected (i.e. not less), but there was no pull-up effect for the more average ability children, and their self-esteem went down. Thus the view of the gifted child as a stimulus to the learning of the more average ability child was not supported. Overall, the study found that the achievements of any pupil were largely independent of those of classmates (unlike HMI 1992 findings), nor did it provide evidence that grouping the gifted together in a normal curriculum was academically beneficial to them, though the researchers felt it *might* be, were the curriculum to be specially designed for them. However, the Canadians, Shore & Delcourt (1996), have said that such research cannot be trusted, and that co-operative learning can be detrimental to the gifted because:

- Their special learning needs are not being met.

- Comparison studies are not adequate enough to investigate this.

- Most research is done with wide variations in the ability of paired children so as to produce more significant results.

- Motivation in the gifted is reduced by denying them regular interaction with ability peers.

In an overview of American research on grouping by ability, Rogers & Span (1993) concluded that for the gifted, streaming improves their achievements, ambitions, critical thinking and creativity, but has little impact on self-esteem. They suggested that it is not so much the group make-up which has these beneficial effects, but the possibilities within the group to enrich or accelerate the curriculum.

In two large studies of young gifted teenagers in Israel, Dar and Resh (1986) investigated the effects of classroom composition on achievement. Their first study was of 700 pupils in the kibbutzim, and the second looked at 4,000 pupils in different kinds of groupings across the country. They concluded that average-ability pupils benefited most from mixed-ability teaching, and the highly able from ability grouping. This was particularly so in some areas, such as "the more hierarchical and abstract segments of the curriculum, namely in subjects like mathematics, some of the exact sciences, and foreign languages" (p.154), as well as special enrichment. Otherwise, they recommended that children be taught together for most lessons.

Aspects of peer-tutoring with differently able young children were investigated in Nottingham (Wood *et al*, 1995). The style of tutoring was found to be different when either a more able or less able child had the greater expertise. Where the high-ability child was the expert he or she taught more, but where the lower-ability child had greater expertise there was more collaboration in learning together. Thus, the make-up of the pair affected the outcome, whether of skills acquisition or conceptual change. But learning together with adults led to even better results for the highly able, notably in encouraging strategic thinking. The researchers suggest emphasis on "contingent instruction", namely that the tutor should immediately offer more help when a learner gets into difficulty, but less when a learner can do the task well. This suggested structuring of learning is in line with Vygotsky's concept of the Zone of Proximal Development (see above).

Effective tutoring by children calls for some maturity. It implies the ability to stand aside from one's own involvement, to provide 'space' for the learner to execute a task: to be able to regulate the learning of others requires the ability to regulate one's own instruction. In general, children who are best at teaching are also best at learning, though quick thinkers can be impatient with slower thinkers. Additionally, although older or more advanced pupils can be very helpful in teaching younger ones, this can be overused so that pupils who are teaching may not be learning during that time (Freeman, 1996b). Reciprocal teaching (Palincsar & Brown, 1984), in which pupils, or pupils and teachers, take turns at teaching, is a useful strategy in mixed-ability situations.

However, even in selective group-work these investigations have shown up problems. For example, the quicker pupils may leap to conclusions too quickly so that the slower ones cannot follow the steps by which these have been reached (if indeed definable steps have been scaled). Although in theory children can change ability groups, they very often stay where they are allocated, a problem for the late-developing potentially able child, who may simply conform to expectations when placed in a lower ability group.

Evidence on the two major types of provision for the very able – acceleration and enrichment – is summarised below. Acceleration is based on the child's already recognised advancement, whereas enrichment can also promote hidden potential. Hence acceleration is reactive while enrichment is proactive. No direct comparisons appear to have been made, though, of how each procedure affects different types of ability.

FORMS OF ACCELERATION

The term "acceleration" is understood variously. Mostly it implies grade-skipping, but for some researchers it can mean individualised provision of any sort which takes the pupils on faster. The many different forms of acceleration are usefully summarised by Montgomery (1996, p.66) and adapted here:

Different forms of acceleration

- Early entry into a new phase of education – from nursery onwards.

- Grade-skipping – promotion above age-peers by one or more years (in America it can be five).

- Subject acceleration – joining more advanced pupils for special subjects.

- Vertical grouping – classes which have wide age ranges of pupils so that the younger one can work with the older ones.

- Out-of-school courses – which give extra lessons in subject areas.

- Concurrent studies – a primary school child may be following a secondary school course etc.

- Compacting studies – the normal syllabus is completed in up to one-third of the time.

- Self-organised study – which the pupils do while the rest of the class is catching up.

- Mentoring – working with an expert in the field, perhaps class teachers or outsiders.

- Correspondence courses.

The cheapest, easiest and most usual form of special provision is to move a bright child up a class or more above his/her age-group: grade-skipping. In National Curriculum terms, the official recommendation is to accelerate stages (see below). But in spite of American evidence that acceleration can work well, it is strongly resisted by teachers and parents in many countries. Perhaps this distrust is because acceleration runs counter to the notion of healthy social development; and maybe it is similar to the distrust of research findings showing that large class sizes have no effect on pupils' achievements. But alternatively, how would a child react if his or her eagerness to learn were held back to the pace of a slower class? And, if the top few per cent are removed to a higher class, does that enable the next brightest to rise to the top and feel better about themselves? Or does taking away the bright ones also take away the stimulation they might bring to the classroom?

The major problem with grade-skipping is that the child 'hurried' on in that way may not be either physically or emotionally mature enough to fit in socially with the older children in the new class. Intellectually, certain subject areas (such as language) require the appropriate life experiences which come with age, and without these the necessary conceptual development may be lacking. Physically, a four-year-old is not as adept as a five-year-old, for instance, and particularly for grade-skipped boys, their apparently late physical development encourages the 'little professor' image of the child as being hopeless at everything which is not school-learning (or music). Research in France compared the self-concepts of secondary children in three groups; 22 who were kept back two years (*double redoublement*), 106 *normal*, and 12 grade-skipped (*avance*), by questionnaire under supervision (Robinson *et al*, 1992). Although there was no difference in self-confidence between the groups, the advanced group were the least well behaved.

The considerable disagreement about whether or not to keep a bright child with age-peers seems to vary with the culture. Whereas some countries, such as Spain or Denmark, do not allow acceleration at all, others only allow it in special circumstances. It is rare in Russia, although there are no prohibitions against it. In China, though, a school may take a child of any age into any stage of education, as long as the child has passed the examinations for that level. There is even provision there for children as young as 12 to attend two of China's technical universities. At both, a five-year course was set up in 1978 to provide for children from across the country, for which about 800 youngsters (mostly boys) applied in 1995, but only 43 were accepted (with an average IQ of 125). To date, 673 early students have graduated, the youngest being 11. Visiting one of the universities, the author's impression was of a high-powered boarding school. The senior tutor there described how the children are well tolerated by the older students, but do not mingle much with them; also that about 15% of the class were introverts and unable to speak their minds. No follow-up studies on the personal effects of this considerable acceleration have been conducted.

Almost all the research evidence promoting the benefits of acceleration is based on studies within the American educational system, where teaching is slower and less differentiated than that in Europe. Indeed, it has been found there that a gifted mathematician can accomplish a whole year's school course in three weeks (Stanley, 1993): would this be equally true in Europe? In some states, whole-class mixed-ability teaching is promoted to the extent that ability or interest grouping is actually prohibited. A report from the (US) Office for Educational Research (OERI, 1993) says that in international comparisons "our youngsters still rank at or near the bottom in all subjects tested" (p.10). This is countered to some extent by special programmes. Even by "1990, 38 states served more than 2 million gifted students", and since then "the number of programs for gifted and talented youngsters has grown substantially" (p. iii). Unfortunately, though, the US is still near the bottom of the comparison list.

In Britain, it is possible not only to accelerate children within the school, but to place pupils in part-time acceleration through higher education institutions. One school, for example, now has 10 pupils on a mathematics foundation course at the Open University in addition to their A-level studies. They are aiming to build up a bank of credits for when they reach university full-time. Israel too has a system for providing advanced pupils with part-time access to higher education, and the first follow-up of 2,495 children (including controls) shows it to be working well, particularly with regard to the pupil's satisfaction, and so it is set to continue (Shahal, 1995).

There is a steady flow of exceptionally advanced pupils in all areas of school work in Britain. In 1988 the Associated Examining Board found that of 493,069 GCE candidates there were 434 O-level entries from pupils under 15, including 30 from children aged 9 - 12. Of 170 A-level candidates under 17, one was aged 11 and another 9. What is more, their results were as good as or better than those of older candidates – at O-level, 35% of entrants under 15 got a grade A, compared with 9% generally, and 11% of young A-level candidates came away with an A, as opposed to 6% of sixth-formers. In their 1995 statistics, there were 43 candidates aged under 15 at A-level standard, but only 7 at GCSE grade (no further breakdown was offered). Unfortunately, we know very little about what sort of schooling and home circumstances produce such results: these precocious examinees have never been investigated.

Germany uses a form of differentiated teaching by school, each type of school aiming for different goals, such as technical or academic. In theory, as pupils develop and change interests they should have the choice of moving from one kind of school to another, and so acceleration is normally considered unnecessary. All the primary and secondary state schools in Lower Saxony were sent questionnaires on their experiences of grade-skipping between 1980 and 1990 (Heinbokel, 1997). The parents, 103 grade-skippers, 20 non grade-skippers and 19 grade-skippers, were interviewed. Almost all the grade-skipping (although only 0.012% of the child population) had taken place in the primary schools. The ratio of girls to boys was 1:6. Reasons given for grade-skipping were usually emotional – boredom, disruptive behaviour (especially in boys) and emotional withdrawal. Although the primary school children were found to be generally happy with the move and coped intellectually in their new class, 14% of the girls and 23% of the boys were reported by parents to have retained their emotional problems. In Hamburg, a secondary school survey of 73 academic and 37 comprehensive schools (77% responded) (Prado & Schiebel, 1995) found that virtually all the grade-skipping took place in the academic-type schools and at all ages. The acceleration was recommended by teachers, and two boys were accelerated for every girl. The social integration process proved to be problematic for some of the accelerated pupils. But this move was always seen as a last resort; most headteachers believed that there were better choices.

There are, in fact, other ways for gifted older children in Germany to exercise their abilities, such as the extremely high-level, fast-growing national competitions in many subjects (e.g. foreign languages and mathematics) which are heavily subsidised by the government (Wagner, 1995). The youngsters are prepared for these in their schools. The prizes are usually of an educational nature, such as payment for a course of the student's choice in any country or subject. Follow-ups are currently being conducted on the effects of these competitions on prize-winners, in particular how they have fared at university.

The success of acceleration in school has been found to be very dependent on the context in which it is done, e.g. the flexibility of the system, how many others in a school are accelerated, the child's level of maturation, and the emotional support provided by the receiving teachers. The age at which the acceleration starts could have different effects, a feature which has not been addressed in the research. In addition, it is often assumed that educational acceleration implies more complex content. However, the child may merely be working along the same lines as before, simply shortening the number of years spent in school. There are times, though, when grade-skipping may be the only option, and when care is taken of the possible problems it has been found to be successful.

But even American research on grade-skipping the gifted (whether defined by IQ or school marks) is divided. The major thrust for it has come from the considerable research in this area headed by Stanley and Benbow who have argued forcefully that acceleration "improves the motivation and scholarship of gifted students" and that fear of emotional and social problems is grossly exaggerated. However, Benbow recognises that acceleration (in any form) is not appropriate for all children, and has outlined factors to take into account when contemplating such action. They include (Benbow, 1991, p. 31):

Only accelerate when:

- There is no pressure to accelerate.
- The pupil is in the top 2 per cent of intelligence.
- The receiving teacher feels positive about it.
- The parents feel positive about it.
- The pupil is advanced in the subject area.
- The pupil is emotionally stable.
- The pupil understands what is involved.
- The pupil wants to be accelerated.

Support for grade-skipping comes from Australia in a 10-year case-study of just 15 children of IQ 160+ (Gross, 1993). Gross wrote somewhat dramatically that these 'profoundly gifted' children had emotional problems because, for them, learning with their age-peers of average ability was like restricting children of average ability to learn with "children who are profoundly intellectually handicapped" (p.475). She was strongly in favour of several grade-skips because "for children of IQ 160 a token grade-skip of one year, even when supplemented with in-class enrichment or pull-out, was no more effective, either academically or socially, than retention in the regular classroom with age-peers" (p. 486). However, in the Freeman (1991) sample which contained 23 youngsters of IQ 160+ in a variety of British schools, IQ was not found to be directly associated with emotional problems.

Even the academic long-term outcomes of acceleration are doubtful. For example, in a ten-year study comparing accelerated and non-accelerated pupils, even the pro-acceleration American researchers, Swiatek and Benbow (1991), found that by age 23 "few significant differences were found between the groups for the individual academic and psycho-social variables studied" (p.528). The most sure effect appeared to be in time saved at school.

The emotional effects of acceleration

In an overview of 26 American studies of acceleration, Kulik and Kulik (1984) found that only a few had investigated the emotional effects, and those had been assessed with paper and pencil tests – "not the methods usually used for measuring success in life" (p.89). Consequently, although the accelerated children had shown good academic progress, no conclusions, they wrote, could be drawn about any other effects of their advancement. Southern & Jones (1991) also found from their wide-ranging review of American research on the effects of acceleration, that the emotional consequences had been neglected by most studies. Nor has there been any research attempting to match pupils with the most appropriate form of acceleration. Yet there is the possibility that the very able might be emotionally more mature than their age-peers. In one study, highly-achieving, intellectually gifted young adolescents were found to be emotionally and intellectually closer to older adolescents than to their age-mates (Luthar *et al*, 1992).

The younger children are, the easier their emotional integration to an older class seems to be, whereas the changes of adolescence can exacerbate differences (Walberg, 1995). Intellectually, too, the effects of accelerated learning have been found to be easier when children are younger.

Begun in 1991, a four-year German experiment compared bright gymnasium (grammar school) pupils who took the Abitur (somewhat like A level) in eight years instead of nine with non-accelerated pupils of the same ability and age (Heller, 1995). The experiment included yearly testing, the provision of feedback to parents, teachers and pupils, and comparing final examination grades. The advanced group felt much more strongly than the non-selected group that their results were due to their own efforts, though they also showed a somewhat higher degree of anxiety. The teachers were found to have difficulties in organising small teaching groups and in promoting co-operation among the pupils. The main conclusion was mixed: primarily that teachers need special training for coping with acceleration; and that this should focus on discovery learning methods, corresponding pupil learning skills and approaches for co-operative learning. Without those special skills, the long-term value for as little as a one-year acceleration would be doubtful.

Most research on acceleration has concentrated on achievement, but self-reports (Freeman, 1996) have provided rare insight into the emotional effects. For the youngsters in the British sample, when a decision had been taken to accelerate it was usually initiated by the teachers with the (sometimes reluctant) agreement of the parents; few of the children had been asked. For 16 of the 17 accelerated children, normal growing-up problems had been decidedly exacerbated by this move – discovered through long home interviews. Both children and parents explained, for example, how difficult it was to cope with a typical problem of how late to stay out, as the older pupils in the accelerated teenager's class were given more freedom. Some of the accelerated youngsters perceived themselves as small, as did their friends, although they were of normal size for their age. The only pupil who was very pleased with the situation was a tall and mature boy, who said it enabled him to leave school earlier. One father said poignantly of his son who had been grade-skipped in a high-powered boys' school by two years: "I felt sorry for him; they were men and he was a boy". A gifted boy commented that if you go to university too young you miss out on so much: "You can't go into the student bar to start with".

The overall conclusion from research is that acceleration can work, particularly for mathematics and second languages, but with very strong caveats. A joint survey between Oxfordshire County Council and Oxford Brookes University of how 12 schools (first, middle and upper) educated their top 2%, found that it was fairly common for first-school pupils to do some work with older pupils when classes were of mixed age, but not otherwise (Oxfordshire, 1995). All the schools provided varied support for their most able children, though what worked in one school might not work in another. But from this and other research in Oxfordshire, the research leader concluded that grade-skipping could be considered as a school's **failure** to provide adequately for its very able pupils (Eyre, 1997).

In a review of American research on emotional development of the accelerated gifted, Cornell *et al* (1991) conclude that "few authors have examined socio-emotional adjustment with adequate psychological measures" (p. 91), and few have looked at the long-term effects. No data have emerged from any study to indicate which students will fare well in early college entrance programmes. The authors issue warnings about drawing pro-acceleration conclusions from studies, which are often carried out by researchers keen on the idea of acceleration but with inadequate concern for the complexities of socio-emotional adjustment. For example, a lack of differences between compared groups may not indicate a lack of problems, but rather the inadequacy of the instruments or methodology. Equally, studies which appear to show the beneficial effects of acceleration do not necessarily demonstrate the negative effects of non-acceleration.

Research on the socio-emotional adjustment of accelerated pupils

- A single measure of self-esteem is inadequate; multiple measures should be used in a developmental context, including family and peers.

- Self-reports can be distorted by defensiveness or lack of awareness. The child has only his or her own experience on which to base feelings and so cannot act as his or her own experimental control.

- Behavioural observation is valuable.

- Standardised tests provide reliable comparisons, but they will not record the special stresses of accelerated pupils, such as losing age-peers. Consequently, they should be used along with individual counselling sessions.

- It is not enough to compare a group of selected accelerated pupils with a non-accelerated group to show the effects of acceleration. Ideally, matched groups of equal ability and achievement should be compared, one staying in the normal classroom and the other accelerated.

- It is useful to assess the emotional development of the children both before and after the acceleration.

- Drop-outs from acceleration should be included in any study; they may be the ones who have experienced the most problems.

Acceleration within specialist schools

Gifted children who have a heightened awareness of the standards of excellence reached by eminent adults may aim higher than their current skills permit, which is particularly frustrating when they have no means of working towards their goals. Some gifts or talents, notably in music and the performing arts, do seem to call for special full-time education so that children can immerse themselves more deeply than in a normal school – and so move on more quickly within their discipline. Being in a specialist school may mean that children can move on individually, in groups or as a class.

There are now 60 experimental primary and middle schools in China with accelerated classes for intellectually gifted pupils of the same age. Keeping the class together is said to remove any emotional problems caused by accelerating above the age group. A comparison study between sixteen-year-olds who had been accelerated as a class was made with a matched group in normal education (reported in Zha 1995a). Using the Chinese version of the Wechsler Intelligence Test, little difference was found in IQ, but a big difference in ways of thinking. Those in the experimental schools were better on tests of memory, attention, spatial and mathematical ability, and consequently learning ability, whereas the others were better in language and the ability to generalise. The gifted in special classes, though, were more often found to have higher aims and were much more competitive (Zha, 1995b).

In Britain there are dozens of 'unofficial' highly selective schools for the academically gifted. Although they are now almost all private, most were originally Direct Grant Schools, some of which became effectively 'hot-houses' for the intellectually gifted in terms of academic success and Oxbridge entrance. These schools often move whole classes up by a year. There are also non-selective maintained schools which specialise in teaching certain subjects to a high level, such as the 222 Technology Colleges and Language Colleges (there are plans for 300 more specialist schools, as reported in TES 1997). These Language Colleges oblige the mixed-ability pupils to take two foreign languages, as distinct from the selective language schools in Russia which teach all subjects in a foreign language. Magnet schools aim to attract (rather than select) talented children to an area of excellence, such as music. Such schools can work like specialist schools in enabling children to learn at their own speed, effectively accelerating them within an accepting school context. However, no research has been done on these group forms of acceleration.

FORMS OF ENRICHMENT

Educational enrichment is the deliberate rounding out of the basic curriculum subjects with ideas and knowledge that enable a pupil to be aware of the wider context of a subject area – not a supplementary diet which depends on whether there is enough money for 'extra' material and tuition. Although it is recommended for all pupils, it is a particularly important aspect of education for those who have the potential to go well beyond the elements of any area of study. The point of enrichment for the highly able is to relate learning to other areas and play with ideas so as to come up with new ones. The teacher's task in enrichment is to provide the groundwork, and to guide and encourage pupils to explore further. The wider gains for the child lie in the advantages of improved understanding, encountering and forming new ideas, along with a possibly enhanced self-concept.

In a survey of 8,000 comparative studies of American education for the gifted, Walberg (1995) found that pupils in enriched education did better in school than equally able children without it. But he stressed that motivation was as important as aptitude. He identified the biblical "Matthew effect" – to them that hath, more will be given – so that the already advanced child is more likely to attract attention and receive extra help and so will improve further. In Israel, special programmes for the gifted (chosen by examinations for general learning ability) serving 12,000 children have been in action for more than 20 years, under the aegis of the Ministry of Education, Culture and Sport. There, in a comparison of 771 children in separate gifted classes in regular schools with 1,008 equally able children who were given a weekly enrichment day, the children in the special classes reported that they were more challenged and did better academically, but also felt isolated from other children (Shahal, 1995). Of those in the enrichment classes, 81% reported problems in making up for the normal work they missed that day, and that this weekly absence caused peer-group problems: most preferred the gifted classes to the general enrichment, as did their parents.

A major problem with enrichment activities for the highly able is that they often lack clear goals. An excellent summary of useful aims for enrichment activities is provided by Hill (in Shore *et al*, 1991, p. 82). These include:

- increasing ability to analyse and solve problems;

- developing profound, worthwhile interests;

- stimulating originality, initiative and self-direction.

Tempest (1974) investigated the effects of one year's enriched teaching (devised by their class-teacher) on a single class of Southport (UK) children selected by high IQ and advanced learning. Their school achievement was compared at the end of the year with that of matched ability children in normal schools. Tempest concluded that most able children could flourish in their normal classrooms if they were taught in a challenging and interesting way. But the gains for the experimental class were not significant, and the follow-up several years later did not show them to have made outstanding progress beyond their ability peers who had not had that enriched education.

A Schoolwide Enrichment Model has been used for 20 years in Connecticut by its designer, Renzulli (1995) and his colleagues – purposely avoiding the label of gifted. This is an interactive model using provision geared to the children's own interests. Renzulli suggested that instead of referring to them as teachers of the gifted, specialists in schools should be called 'enrichment specialists', to assist all teachers of all subjects in the promotion of talent development. The procedure has been found to be particularly helpful to developing the aptitudes of bright children from deprived backgrounds – a form of identification through provision. The programme suggests modifications to the regular curriculum which would be supplemented by group counselling, mentorships, the use of other educational resources and agencies, and so on. These are included in the list of suggestions on enrichment below.

Findings from Purdue University, USA, suggest that taking selected pupils out of class for special teaching should not be a voluntary after-school extra, but should be integrated with the normal school curriculum. A pull-out Program for Academic Enrichment was investigated after 10 years (Moon *et al*, 1994). The 23 youngsters and their families who had been involved for at least three years were questioned in a case-study approach. Although the teachers had been trained for this work, they were given considerable leeway in what they did, which made outcome comparisons difficult. Results indicated that the gifted pass through different stages of talent development, and so any provision is at its most effective if it is in tune with their development. However, this enrichment programme had only moderate long-term effects; the extra progress the children had made mostly settled back to that of their peers who had not had these experiences.

Overall, the research shows that improved adult outcomes, in terms of eminence, resulting from specially enriched childhood education are uncertain. For example, by the ages of 40 to 50, not one of a sample of 210 New York children selected for the Hunter School for the Gifted by their high-IQ scores (mean IQ 157) had reached eminence, in spite of their broad, rich education (Subotnik *et al*, 1993). The researchers suggested:

Possible reasons why children with an enriched gifted education did not reach eminence

- An exceptionally high IQ is not enough to predict eminence.

- Educating for eminence is not itself a feasible goal.

- A generally enriched education does not appear to be sufficient to enable high-IQ children to reach world-class standards. Instead, their education should have high academic standards and provide opportunities for scholarship in the areas of the children's interests.

- The children did not aim for eminence, either because they had been labelled gifted and so did not need to prove their high ability level, or because they chose to avoid the distress of aiming for the top and settled for relatively happy successful lives.

Some ways of organising enrichment

- *In-service courses and workshops:* for teachers to assist enrichment in the normal classroom.

- *Formal teaching can be loosened:* with a willingness to alter routine. This could be by restructuring the school timetable to include periods of independent learning, possibly carried out less formally at the instigation of individual teachers. For example, if the geography teacher has noticed that her top few pupils seem to be eager to get on with the subject, she should be able to approach the head and other members of staff to suggest that they be allowed to work (either in the geography room or outside it) on specific projects. She would have to know that they knew the current work well, and that what she set them to do was not simply more of the same, but was rather of a compatible and enriching nature.

- *Contact with professionals:* children can benefit through interactions with e.g. artists, performers, agricultural and industrial scientists, scholars, craftspeople and others who are not primarily educators. This could be via assigning pupils to personal mentors (see Freeman, 1998).

- *Extra enrichment material:* can be shared by a group of schools, or housed in the school library so that a child can be given permission to go out of the classroom to use it. Enriched curricular materials need not be directly related to the lesson, and are useful for times when children finish assignments early, or simply to provide a challenge. Carefully chosen commercial toys and games can be as helpful as materials specifically designed to increase young children's skills of observation and planning.

- *Enrichment support systems:* these will obviously vary with the community. There may be local associations, or clubs and societies which run activities and would welcome school groups, such as those for talented children or young mathematicians. There may be museum and library courses, such as art or poetry sessions for children at weekends, even correspondence courses, and museums, exhibition centres, arts galleries etc. often have dedicated educational staff eager to assist.

- *Competitions:* run by private groups, such as newspaper poetry competitions, or international ones such as the Odyssey of the Mind, which are open to all children as competitors.

- *Colleges or other places of higher-level education:* may be persuaded to allow bright children to use their facilities, while businesses and places of production may also be willing to help.

- *Modify the regular curriculum:* the challenge level of the learning material should be differentiated through, e.g. curriculum compacting and grouping of pupils with similar interests.

- *Increase in-depth learning and the promotion of higher-order skills:* especially of real-world problems, increasing social consciousness.

- *Out of school sessions:* can be run by specialised teachers and outside experts and for different lengths of time, whether an hour or a day. This part-time system may avoid the side-effect of upsetting the others in the class or affecting the selected ones emotionally, while giving the very able pupils an opportunity to work at their own pace with others of the same ability and interests. The weaknesses of such pull-out activities, though, include fragmentation of learning, disruption of classes, and missed lessons.

High-level creativity

From the sample of evidence presented above, it can be seen that although a pupil may achieve extremely well in school examinations or score very highly on an IQ test, he or she may not take that learning further in terms of creative thinking and discovery, possibly because of the pressure to score highly in examinations. Imagination and creativity are difficult to measure. Imagination is to a large extent the precursor of creativity: the outcome of imagination could be, for example, new conclusions from mentally rearranging what is already known, which often precedes creative scientific advancement (Simonton, 1988). Overviewing research on creativity testing, Cropley (1995) found that predicting future creativity from tests is little better than predicting it from IQ, but it is greatly improved by focusing on particular areas such as music or creative writing. He suggests that such tests are still useful, though, as indicators of potential because it is not normally until adulthood that creative products can be widely acclaimed.

But can high-achieving pupils be taught to be creative, would it benefit their lives, and is enrichment the means to do this? As creative thinking is part of everyday thinking, there is no apparent reason why this approach to learning cannot be taught. In fact, Torrance (1987), who has worked for many years in this area, examined 142 American creativity courses and concluded that there was ample evidence that it can be taught through different kinds of enriched teaching. The best, he found, involved encouraging creative thinking skills and developing the child's motivation to experiment with ideas.

Urban (1995), a German researcher in the area of gifted creativity, concludes that it is difficult to separate intellect and creativity in very young children, but that as social and educational pressures impose order on their "chaotic" thinking processes, the distinction becomes easier. He has constructed a (Compotential) model which does not measure creativity as such, but rather 'image production' and the psychological aspects of creativity. On this basis, he suggests that it is important to help pupils see the value of creative solutions in real life situations, and that the development of a creative approach to all learning and action should be seen as a long-term process incorporating personal involvement. Indeed, creativity in all its forms is described by the American Weisberg (1992) as expertise combined with a high level of motivation.

In line with this, it has been seen that culture and opportunity can make a big difference to creativity. A three-year comparative study on technical creativity with highly able German and Chinese young adolescents (Heller & Hany, 1995) found that initially the Chinese scored more highly than the Germans for scientific knowledge and non-verbal tests, whereas the Germans were better on the practical tasks. For both nationalities girls were less competent at solving scientific and technical problems, particularly the German girls who had tried to compensate for their less good spatial reasoning by using other types of less efficient thinking. The general conclusions were that for both countries, age, intelligence and sex were the main determinants of technical creativity, but in the end it was the individual's belief that they were able to succeed which provided the vital foundation for success.

Most researchers on this subject, such as those mentioned above, are in agreement that the essentials for high-level creativity are:

The essentials for creativity

- Motivation

- Knowledge

- Opportunity

- Creative teaching style

- Encouragement to be creative

- Acceptance of one's own personality

- The courage to be different

Several of these may be in short supply for able high achievers in pressured schooling (Freeman, 1991; Sternberg & Lubart,1995). But precise methods of teaching for creativity, at whatever level and whether general or specific, have yet to be defined precisely and reliably. Some psychologists, such as Eysenck (1995), find that a high IQ score is at the root of all creative genius, but most others believe that creative success cannot be separated from social forces, such as encouragement and motivation. Kaufman (1992), in her follow-up of American Presidential Scholars, found that the only creative way in which those individuals used their vast memory banks was as props for their self-esteem!

The Assisted Places Scheme

The Assisted Places Scheme in Britain was set up in 1981 to pay private school fees for able children, but no more scholars were taken from 1997. Over 75,000 pupils have received such assistance from public funds at a cost of over £150 million per annum, serving 1% of the school population, and those who have started will continue to be funded until they leave school, for up to nine years. Financial assistance is scaled, depending on parental income, but some private schools are still being supported in this way by about 50% of their pupils. Research on pupil uptake (Edwards *et al*, 1989) found that fewer than 10% of selected children had fathers who were manual workers, compared with 50% in service-class occupations, such as teaching. Although children from single-parent families made up the largest category, other disadvantaged groups, notably the unemployed, and black and Asian families, had poor representation. They also found that two-thirds of those taking up places for the first time at 16 were already fee-paying pupils in the same school.

Pupils who had won Assisted Places were matched on verbal reasoning scores only, and comparisons made between the examination results of those who had taken up the places and those who had not (West & West, 1997). The takers were found to have done significantly better at A level and in more subjects than those who had rejected the offer and taken their A levels in the state sector. Questionnaires were sent to 62 participating schools (response rate 87%), but the comparison groups were small and unbalanced – 334 takers and 59 non-takers. There were 34% girls and 66% boys (the same gender proportions as in most studies of able children selected by teachers).

The researchers, moreover, had no direct communication with the pupils or their families, so there was no way of knowing why any child had declined the free private school place, nor did they know which schools had refused to answer or why. They may, for example, have had worse examination results, or taken pupils from different backgrounds. But more importantly, these results are only indicative because, as the researchers explained: "the possibility cannot be ruled out that the advantage for AP pupils arises from factors other than their education in the independent sector (e.g. family background and parental involvement)" (p.287). Indeed, research by Saunders (1996) at Sussex University based on the life progress of 17,000 adults found that private schooling had little or no effect on their eventual job prospects, and concluded that whatever your social class: "in the end, what matters most is whether you are bright and whether you work hard" (p. 72).

A 1997 Mori Poll commissioned by ISIS (Independent Schools Information Service) looked at the "social group, household income and ethnic background of the children" who obtained an Assisted Place. A random selection of 44 schools were asked to fill in a form providing information on their Assisted Places pupils. Forms were received back from 34 schools, a response rate of 77%, yielding information on 3,897 pupils, just over 10% of the total in assisted places. They concluded "While those from the higher socio-economic groups (ABC1) are just as likely to benefit from participating in the Assisted Places Scheme as they were in 1991 [a previous Mori poll], they are more likely to receive financial support (+8 points)". This appears to mean that although the proportion of higher socio-economic groups has not changed, their income has dropped so drastically that they are awarded a much higher level of funding from the scheme. Additionally, although 71% of group A and B parents were aware of the scheme, only 29% of D and E parents knew of it.

There are, however, questions which one might ask about the Mori research, such as which parent's income was used as the criterion? If parents were divorced or the mother was working part-time, using her income could diminish the apparent finance available to the child. If, as Edwards claimed seven years ago, two-thirds of those taking up places for the first time at 16 were *already* fee-paying pupils in the school for which they won the Assisted Place, these figures are unlikely to be radically changed. How was the pupil paid for and by whom, *before* they gained an Assisted Place? Although the report claimed that the proportion of ethnic minority pupils had risen to 11%, these were mostly from Asian families, and 15% of the pupils could not be identified. The main point of concern is that as it was usually the maintained schools that had brought these scholars to the point of success in obtaining the Assisted Place, why then were they being removed from the maintained sector?

Vacation courses and out-of-school activities for the very able

By far most of the special provision for gifted children takes place in North America, usually as holiday courses, whether daily or live-in. The numbers of these have grown since they started in the late 1970s to cater for many thousands of bright 12–16 year-olds. The three largest organisations offering these courses are the Center for Talented Youth at Johns Hopkins University (a branch is at City University, Dublin), the Talent Identification Programme at Duke University and the Northwestern Center for Talent Development. They each have extensive data comparing the achievements of students on their courses, who were selected by scores on Scholastic Aptitude Tests (American SATs), with those who failed to gain a place. The researches virtually all show the courses to have increased the students' knowledge and enthusiasm for the areas studied.

The German SchulerAkademien (pupil academies run by Bildung und Begabung, a charitable foundation for the gifted) are nationwide high-powered courses and competitions. Since 1988 more than 15,000 highly academic and highly motivated 16-19 year-olds have attended for about 17 days with about 90 participants on each course (Wagner, 1995). An evaluation study of one of these courses revealed the participants' academic profiles: their IQs were 15 points above that of the average gymnasium (grammar school) student, and they enjoyed music most and physical education least (Wagner *et al*, 1995). At the end of the course, boys and girls equally were better able to control their own learning at both general and specific levels, and they improved on their already strong co-operative learning attitudes.

By chance, it was possible to make a valid comparison with non-attenders at the SchulerAkademien when one of the vacation courses was so oversubscribed that the final criterion of acceptance by identically able teenagers was the luck of the draw. Those who took the intensive learning course were found to have benefited from it academically. However, the organiser, Dr. Harald Wagner, told the writer that by far the greatest benefits to the youngsters were social. This is in accord with the findings of a wide American survey, that although the educational value of provision on courses was very variable, it did consistently provide opportunities for the gifted to interact socially with others like themselves (Cox *et al*, 1985).

In Israel, the Weizmann Institute runs residential summer programmes using mentors, as well as a 'Maths by Mail' arrangement which teaches up to 2,000 primary schoolchildren annually (Maoz, 1993). Research has shown that the students who enrol are keen to learn, and enjoy science instruction which is different from school and 'real'. The leisure time activities of such students are more varied than those of non-participating peers of equal ability.

Highly able children who take part in special summer and weekend schools often describe their pleasure at meeting and relaxing with others of their own kind. In Britain, several local authorities and a few private organisations (e.g. National Association for Gifted Children, Gift, Children of High Intelligence) run out-of-school activities, but no data has ever been collected on the outcomes. In his overview of international provision for the gifted, Heller (1995) found that valid comparisons between different programmes of special provision on matched-ability highly able children are extremely rare, if they exist at all. However, it is not unreasonable to guess that bright motivated youngsters, under intensive tutoring in an exciting atmosphere of learning, would indeed become more proficient learners.

TEACHER EXPERTISE

Faced with pupils who read voraciously, reason and absorb information rapidly, ask questions, invent problems, provide creative solutions, and cope with concepts and abstract ideas from a young age, some teachers may feel inadequate. But a teacher does not have to be super-knowledgeable to work with highly able children, rather he or she needs to be interested and keen to learn along with the pupils. All teachers can offer support and expertise to their highly able pupils. In America, however, teachers of the gifted must be certified as such in 21 of the 50 states, and a survey found that the trained teachers were more effective (Hansen & Feldhusen, 1994). It could be expected that teachers with a positive attitude to the highly able and the techniques to help them would be more effective, and with training would be even more so.

Differences have been found in Britain between the attitudes and teaching of primary and secondary school teachers (Kerry & Kerry, 1997). Teachers attending training sessions on the education of the very able were questioned about their strategies for differentiated teaching with a checklist they compiled themselves. Although the research was small and focused on already interested teachers (58 responses), it does provide an indication of "thoughtful practice". All the teachers favoured asking open questions, demanding higher targets, encouraging library skills, and conducting one-to-one discussions with pupils. But in addition, primary schools used more demanding resources and more open-ended tasks. Differentiation by tasks was underused in secondary schools.

The academic learning of the very able can be enhanced by a well-planned and executed education system suitable for their needs. Wider support, especially family support, is essential for pupils to reach the highest levels of thought and creativity. Recommendations from the research are presented overleaf.

Teaching the very able in the normal classroom

Improving task demand

- New knowledge should not be presented in isolation as facts to be remembered, but given within the context of a conceptual framework.

- The teacher should take a problem-posing as well as a problem-solving approach to stimulate thinking about the study area.

- Teach for clear 'scientific' thinking skills to greater depth than normal.

- Emphasise abstract as well as basic concepts.

- Materials should be high in quality, and reading levels should demand complex responses and avoid repetition.

Using language

- The intellectual demands of a lesson can be recognised by the level, speed, and quality of the verbal interactions that go on in it.

- The talented should also use the appropriate technical language, rather than a simplified version.

- Encourage play with words, especially proverbs and idioms.

- Encourage questioning as a part of everyday learning, to stimulate thinking and creative problem-solving

Communication

- E.g. pupils explaining out loud, comparing old and new learning and ideas with ability-peers.

- Teach research skills so that pupils can expand on material for themselves.

Encouragement to excellence

- Own-time rewards. When children get top marks consistently they can be rewarded with time for their own projects, in accord with a contract which the teacher draws up. For example, the time must be spent on a project which has been agreed, the child may not interrupt the rest of the class, this time may be spent in the library, all own-time work must be looked at by the teacher.

- Goals should be set to a high, perhaps professional standard.

- Mentors should be appointed where possible.

- Make sure that creative abilities are nurtured.

- See that projects are completed before the next rush of enthusiasm for something new, and that work is checked.

From the administrative perspective, social and political attitudes appear to be far more important than the availability of resources in recognising and providing for the special needs of very able pupils. In some rich countries such as Sweden and Denmark it is not acceptable to provide differently for pupils who show evidence of higher-level potential than others (though this is now being reconsidered) (Persson, 1998). In China and the former USSR, high-level achievement has traditionally been viewed as valuable to society rather than the individual. Every year, Americans spend many millions of dollars from government and other sources on research and programmes in gifted education, which is why the vast majority of research findings and theories come from there. Although there is now a steady flow of research and some theory coming from other countries, particularly Germany and Israel, very little research is generated in this area in Britain.

The new National Curriculum

When the debate on the National Curriculum started in the 1970s, the concern was mainly with the need to raise basic standards, and consequently, before the 1994 review, very able children were not specifically mentioned. Now, however, there is the 'Access' statement (below) which appears in the introduction to each of the Subject Orders in the Revised National Curriculum (issued in January 1995 and put into effect August 1995). It is somewhat confusing, though, because in the same statement the suggestion is made that an able pupil can work at key stages which may be different from the rest of the class, and yet he or she should remain within the context of the pupil's age. Teachers are to make the decisions themselves on how to meet their able pupils' needs, drawing on evidence from research to make their judgements.

The access statement

> "For the small number of pupils who may need the provision, material may be selected from earlier or later key stages where this is necessary to enable individual pupils to progress and demonstrate achievement. Such material should be presented in contexts suitable to the pupil's age."

In addition, each Attainment Target within each National Curriculum subject has a level description for 'exceptional performance' which "is available for very able pupils and to help teachers differentiate exceptional performance at Key Stage 3". The new slimmer curriculum, in all but the basics of English, maths and science, should also enable schools to better meet the needs of their more able pupils as there is now more space in the timetable to provide necessary learning extensions.

The National Curriculum is supposed to bring advantages for the more able in that it has "... concentrated attention on the need for differentiation of work for pupils of different abilities, and its procedures for assessment, recording and reporting on pupils' knowledge, skills and understanding have helped to focus more sharply on the achievements and progress of the more able" (DFE, 1993, p.9). However, the National Curriculum is premised on

LIVERPOOL JOHN MOORES UNIVERSITY
LEARNING SERVICES

children's regular developmental sequence, which is unlikely to take into account the research findings that many very able children have an unusual style of development.

Recognising the need for differentiation is indeed excellent, but as the research outlined above has shown, using measured achievement as the basic means of recognition would miss much undeveloped potential. Bearing in mind the research described above on teacher identification of the very able: "The Secretary of State proposes to place *sole* [my emphasis] reliance on teacher assessment for the award of levels to exceptionally able pupils; to discontinue the extension tests accordingly; and to ask SCAA (School Curriculum and Assessment Authority) to investigate how exceptional performance might be recognised" (DfEE, 1996, p.4). For the time being, National Curriculum assessment is to be **summate** – a brief summary of how a child stands in relation to others – and **formative/diagnostic** – with future progress in mind. However, the assessment procedures of the National Curriculum are still under review.

In May 1995, the Office for Standards in Education published reviews of primary (first year) and secondary (second year) state school inspection findings for teachers in 12 specific subjects; only a few of them refer to high ability. There is no reference to the very able in history, music, art or physical education, for example. One OFSTED report which does, though, is on mathematics (Askew & Wiliam, 1995). The authors describe how "It is rare for attention to be given to the needs of able pupils other than by placing them in 'top' sets" (p.18). Almost all reference to the highly able is in terms of advanced school achievement, and most notably the possibility of accelerating pupils more quickly through courses, such as by sitting examinations early, and even devising personalised timetables to speed up knowledge acquisition. However, the above evidence shows that there are many other effective ways of helping the very able.

Possible benefits for able children from the National Curriculum

- Affirmation for teachers that their assessments are of equal value to test results, and will be given equal prominence in reports, which enables their sensitivity to be used. Time constraints make it difficult, though, for teachers to make careful diagnoses when test scripts are returned to them in the last three weeks of the summer term.

- Emphasis on cross-curricular work, which supports the theory of transfer of learning.

- The new National Curriculum indicates that more research and project-based activity is welcome, although emphasis is heavily knowledge-based.

A policy in every school

Some schools and a handful of LEAs do have a policy for the education of their brightest pupils, even though no specific suggestions or obligations are offered within the National Curriculum. The partnership of parents, teachers, and the children themselves is essential in changing administrative policy and putting such a policy into action (see Freeman, 1995b and Eyre, 1997 for details on a school policy for the highly able). The increasing number of British schools expressing concern for the very able is probably due to:

(a)   Government guidance, DfEE conferences and free publications

(b)   OFSTED inspections

(c)   The NACE/DFE project, 'Supporting the Education of Able Pupils in Maintained Schools'. This was carried out for three years starting in 1993 with the teacher organisation the National Association for Able Children in Education (NACE) in England and Wales. It involved 20,000 teachers in 37 LEAs, and resulted in a measured increase in LEAs with specific policies.

(d)   Others who have also been active in training teachers of the highly able, such as the (parent based) National Association for Gifted Children, the commercial venture, Gift, and individuals. However, there has never been any evaluation or follow-up of their work.

A school's policy for its brightest pupils is an indication of how it attends to the different educational requirements of all its children. The following two major points summarise practical aspects, arising from the research, of a policy which a school can incorporate for the encouragement of high-level performance in both pupils and teachers:

The commitment of the headteacher. The leadership attitude he or she gives in the education of the school's brightest pupils should provide an immediate incentive for teachers. But to offer more than fine intentions, the headteacher has to make practical support available in the distribution of resources, as well as with e.g. flexibility of timetables, response to noise levels in the classroom, quality and quantity of work that is completed and attitudes to parents. The influence of the head provides encouragement and support for curricular and instructional innovations.

A whole-school approach. All the school staff should be involved in presenting a policy, since if potentially able children spend time with disinterested teachers rather than with those motivated to help them they may not be encouraged to move ahead. Teachers should be aware of their own attitudes to the highly able, and be helped to understand why they may feel that such children can look after themselves. They may need reminding that a school should cater fairly for the needs of all its pupils, and that the potentially gifted need interaction at a higher level of challenge. The school climate has to favour excellence in all its pupils' efforts, extended where possible and frequently acknowledged (such as in exhibitions).

It is useful to have one or more staff members, preferably with some extra status, who can act as co-ordinators for the talented across the whole curriculum. This role may be seen as one component of the school's obligation to its brightest pupils, to monitor and evaluate the education they receive; this should be a position of special responsibility, co-ordinating with heads of departments.

The Education Act of 1981 defined pupils with special educational needs as those who require provision beyond that which is normally provided by the school. In Britain, the need for an appropriate education for the very able is becoming recognised, although this is far from evenly spread across education authorities.

It is clear from the research that such education must be supported by suitably trained teachers, informed parents, and the pupils themselves. No single style of programme, though, can be expected to cater for the needs of all very able pupils, and there is also the possibility of the well-known (Hawthorne) effect of raised productivity following *any* change in education. But the evidence points to the benefits of focusing on particular educational provision for the very able. Neither general enrichment nor simple grade-skipping are adequate as blanket measures.

High-level potential can be developed in schools through these two somewhat overlapping routes:

- **differentiation** – the appropriate match between the curriculum, the content and the characteristics of the pupil;

- **individualisation** – where the pupil has greater responsibility for the content and pace of his or her own educational progress. In this, children would be required to monitor their own learning.

Above all, there can be no appropriate education for the very able without sufficient, if not generous, provision of learning materials and teaching. This is particularly true for pupils who do not have access to such facilities and encouragement outside school. The dominant current concern of research into the education of the very able is the interaction between the child's potential and the provision to develop it. Without that dynamic element, we return to the old ideas of fixed abilities, most notably intelligence. In Britain, most of what is needed to develop every child's potential is already in place. Using the example of school sport - The Sports Approach - less popular subjects, such as chemistry, French, or business studies could be supported with similar generosity. We could then expect to see a great rise in the proportion of pupils we now recognise as very able.

Adey, P. (1991), 'Pulling yourself up by your own thinking', *European Journal for High Ability, 2*, 28-34.

Adreani, O. D. & Pagnin, A. (1993), 'Nurturing the moral development of the gifted', in K.A. Heller, F.J. Monks & A.H. Passow, *International Handbook of Research and Development of Giftedness and Talent.* Oxford: Pergamon Press.

Albert, R. S. (Ed.) (1992). *Genius and Eminence: the Social Psychology of Creativity and Exceptional Achievement,* (second edition) Oxford: Pergamon Press.

Ari, B.A. & Rich, Y. (1992), 'Meeting the educational needs of all students in the heterogeneous class', in P.S. Klein and A. J. Tannenbaum (Eds.) *To Be Young and Gifted.* New Jersey: Ablex Publishing.

Arnold, K. D. & Subotnik, R.F. (1994), 'Lessons from contemporary longitudinal studies', in R.F. Subotnik, & K.D. Arnold, (Eds.) (1994) *Beyond Terman: contemporary longitudinal studies of giftedness and talent.* New Jersey: Ablex Publishing.

Arnold, K.D. (1995), *Lives of Promise: What Becomes of High School Valedictorians?* San Francisco: Jossey-Bass.

Arnot, M. David, M. & Weiner, G. (1996). *Educational Reforms and Gender Equality in Schools.* Manchester: EOC.

Askew, M. & Wiliam, D. (1995). *Recent Research in Mathematics Education 5-16.* London: HMSO.

Babaeva, J.D. (1996). 'Psychological training for revealing of "hidden" giftedness', in Leites, N.S. (Ed.). *Psychology of Children Giftedness and Youth.* Moscow, Academia, pp.158-177.

Babaeva, J.D. (1998 in press). 'The dynamic theory of giftedness: conception and practice', *High Ability Studies, 9.2.*

Bakker, D.J. (1990). *Neuropsychological Treatment of Dyslexia.* Oxford: Oxford University Press.

Benbow, C.P. & Lubinski, D. (1993), 'Psychological profiles of the mathematically talented: some sex differences and evidence supporting their biological basis', in Bock, G.R. & Ackrill, K.A. *The Origins and Development of High Ability* (Ciba Foundation Symposium). Chichester: Wiley.

Benbow, C.P. (1988). 'Sex differences in mathematical reasoning ability in intellectually talented pre-adolescents: their nature, effects and possible causes'. *Behavioural and Brain Sciences, 11*, 169-232.

Benbow, C.P. (1991). 'Meeting the needs of gifted students through use of acceleration', in M.C. Wang, M.C. Reynolds and H.J. Walberg (Eds.) *Handbook of Special Education.* Vol. 2. New York: Pergamon Press.

Benn, C. & Chitty, C. (1996). *Thirty Years On: Is Comprehensive Education Alive and Well or Struggling to Survive?* London: David Fulton.

Bennett, N., Desforges, C., Cockburn, A. & Wilkinson, B. (1984). *The Quality of Pupils' Learning Experiences.* Hove: Lawrence Earlbaum.

Berry, C., (1990). 'On the origins of exceptional intellectual and cultural achievement', in Michael J. A. Howe (Ed.), *Encouraging the Development of Exceptional Skills and Talents.* Leicester: British Psychological Society.

Bloom, B.S. (1985). *Developing Talent in Young People*, New York: Ballantine Books.

Boekaerts, M. (1991). 'The affective learning process and giftedness', *European Journal for High Ability*, 2, 146-160.

Boncori, L. (1996), 'A longitudinal study on academic success and satisfaction'. Paper given at the 5th conference of the European Council for High Ability, Vienna.

Bouchard, T.J. (1997), 'IQ similarity in twins reared apart: findings and responses to critics', in *Intelligence, Heredity and Environment*, R.J. Sternberg & E. Grigorenko (Eds.) Cambridge: Cambridge University Press.

Brody, L.E. & Persson Benbow C. (1986). 'Social and emotional adjustment of adolescents extremely talented in verbal or mathematical reasoning'. *Journal of Youth and Adolescence, 15*, 1-18

Brumbaugh, K., Marchaim, U. & Litto, F.M. (1994). 'How should Developing Countries plan for and implement educational technology: one example.' Conference proceedings, *11th International Conference on Technology and Education*, London, March 27-30. p. 43-45.

Butler-Por, N. (1993). 'Underachieving gifted students', in K.A. Heller, F.J. Monks & A.H. Passow, *International Handbook of Research and Development of Giftedness and Talent*. Oxford: Pergamon Press.

Chyriwsky, M. & Kennard, R. (1997), 'Attitudes to able children; a survey of mathematics teachers in English secondary schools'. *High Ability Studies*, 8, 47-59.

Colangelo, N. & Assouline, S. (1995), 'Self-concept of gifted students: patterns by self-concept domain, grade level, and gender', in M.W. Katzko and F.J. Monks (Eds.) *Nurturing Talent; Individual Needs and Social Ability*. Assen, NL: Van Gorcum.

Cornell, D.G., Callahan, C.M., Bassin, L.E. & Ramsay, S.G. (1991), 'Affective development in accelerated students', in W. T. Southern & E.D. Jones *The Academic Acceleration of Gifted Children*. New York: Teacher's College.

Cornell, D.G., Delcourt, M.A.B., Bland, L.C., Goldberg, M.G. & Oram, G., (1994) 'Low incidence of behaviour problems among elementary school students in gifted programs', *Journal for the Education of the Gifted*, 18, 4-19.

Cox, J., Daniel, N., & Boston, B.A. (1985). *Educating Able Learners: Programs and Promising Practices*. Austin: University of Texas Press.

Cropley, A.J. (1995), 'Creative intelligence: a concept of "true" giftedness', in J. Freeman, P. Span, & H. Wagner (Eds.). *Actualising Talent: a Life-span Approach*. London: Cassell.

Csikszentmihalyi, M., Rathunde, K. & Whalen, S. (1993). *Talented Teenagers. The Roots of Success and Failure*. Cambridge: Cambridge University Press.

Czeschlik, T. & Rost, D.H. (1995), 'Sociometric types and children's intelligence'. *British Journal of Developmental Psychology*, 13, 177-189.

Dahme, G. (1996), 'Teachers' conceptions of gifted students in Indonesia (Java), Germany and USA'. Paper given at the 5th conference of the European Council for High Ability, Vienna.

Dar, Y. & Resh, N. (1986) *Classroom Composition and Pupil Achievement: a Study of the Effects of Ability-based Classes*. London: Gordon and Breach.

Denton, C. & **Postlethwaite, K.** (1985). *Able Children: Identifying them in the Classroom*, Windsor: NFER-Nelson.

Department for Education (1993). *Exceptionally Able Children*. London: Department for Education.

Deslisle, J.R. (1992). *Guiding the Social and Emotional Development of Gifted Youth*. London: Longman.

DfEE (1996). *Review of Assessment and Testing Consultation Paper*. London: DfEE.

DfEE/SCAA (1994). DfEE/SCAA Consultation Conferences on Assessment and Testing: Summary Report. (SCAA\96002\1)

Dujardin, K., Guerrien, A., & **Leconte, P.** (1990). 'Sleep, brain activation and cognition'. *Physiol. Behav.* 47,1271-78.

Edwards, T. Fitz, J. & **Whitty, G.** (1989). *The State and Private Education: an Evaluation of the Assisted Places Scheme*. Brighton: The Falmer Press.

Elshout, J. (1995) 'Talent: the ability to become an expert', in J. Freeman, P. Span, & H. Wagner (Eds.) *Actualising Talent: a Lifelong Challenge*. London: Cassell.

Emerick, L.J. (1992), 'Academic underachievement among the gifted: Students perceptions of factors that reverse the pattern'. *Gifted Child Quarterly*, 36, 140-146.

Ericsson, K.A. & **Lehman, A.C.** (1996). 'Expert and exceptional performance: evidence of maximal adaptation to task constraints'. *Annual Review of Psychology*, 47, 273-305.

Eyre, D. (1997). *Able Children in Ordinary Schools*. London: David Fulton.

Eysenck, H.J. (1995) *Genius: the Natural History of Creativity*. Cambridge: Cambridge University Press.

Farrell, D.M. (1989), 'Suicide among gifted students', *Roeper Review*, 11, 134-139.

Feldhusen, J.F. & **Kroll, M.D.,** (1991), 'Boredom or challenge for the academically talented in school', *Gifted Education International*, 7, 80-81.

Feldman, D.H. with **Goldsmith L.T.** (1986) *Nature's Gambit: Child Prodigies and the Development of Human Potential*. New York: Basic Books.

Feuerstein, R. & **Tannenbaum, A.J**. (1993). 'Mediating the learning experience of gifted underachievers', in B. Wallace & H.B. Adams, *Worldwide Perspectives on the Gifted Disadvantaged*. (Ed.) Bicester: AB Academic Publishers.

Flynn, J.R. (1991). *Asian Americans: Achievement Beyond IQ*. London: Erlbaum.

Freeman, J. (1991). *Gifted Children Growing Up*. London: Cassell; Portsmouth, N.H.: Heinemann Educational.

Freeman, J. (1992). 'Boredom, high ability and underachievement', in V. Varma (Ed.) *How and Why Children Fail*. London: Jessica Kingsley.

Freeman, J. (1993), 'Parents and families in nurturing giftedness and talent', in K.A. Heller, F.J. Monks, A. H. Passow (Eds.) *International Handbook for Research on Giftedness and Talent*. Oxford: Pergamon Press.

Freeman, J. (1995), 'Towards a policy for actualizing talent', in J. Freeman, P. Span, & H. Wagner (Eds.) *Actualizing Talent: a Lifelong Challenge*. London: Cassell.

Freeman, J. (1996a). *Highly Able Girls and Boys*. London: Department for Education and Employment.

Freeman, J. (1996b) 'Self reports on research in high ability', *High Ability Studies, 7*, 191-201.

Freeman, J. (1997) 'The emotional development of the highly able'. *European Journal of Psychology in Education. XII*, 479-493.

Freeman, J. (1998) 'Mentoring gifted pupils', in S. Goodlad (Ed.) *Mentoring and Tutoring by Students*. London: Kogan Page.

Gagné, F. (1985), 'Giftedness and talent', *Gifted Child Quarterly*, 29, 103-112.

Gagné, F. (1995), 'Learning about the nature of gifts and talents through peer and teacher nominations', in M.W. Katzko and F.J. Monks (Eds.) *Nurturing Talent; Individual Needs and Social Ability*. Assen, NL: Van Gorcum.

Gallagher, J., Harraine, C.C. & Coleman, M.R. (1997), 'Challenge or boredom? Gifted students' views on their schooling'. *Roeper Review, 19*, 132-136.

Galloway, G. (1994), 'Psychological studies of the relationship of sense of humour to creativity and intelligence: a review', *European Journal for High Ability, 5*, 133-144.

Gardner, H. (1983) *Frames of Mind: the Theory of Multiple Intelligences*. New York: Basic Books.

Gardner, H. (1993). *Creating Minds: an Anatomy of Creativity seen through the lives of Freud, Einstein, Picasso, Stravinsky, Eliot, Graham, and Gandhi*. New York: Basic Books.

Gardner, H. (1997). *Extraordinary Minds*. London: Weidenfeld and Nicolson.

George, D. (1992). *The Challenge of the Able Child*. London: David Fulton.

Goertzel, M.G., Goertzel, V., and Goertzel, T.G. (1978). *300 Eminent Personalities*. San Francisco: Jossey Bass.

Golombok, S. & Fivush, R. (1994). *Gender Development*. Cambridge: Cambridge University Press.

Good, T.L. (1966), 'Teacher expectations', in E. de Corte & F.E. Weinert (Eds.) *International Encyclopedia of Developmental and Instructional Psychology*. Oxford: Pergamon.

Gottfried, A.W., Gottfried, A.E., Bathurst, K. & Guerin, D.W. (1994). *Gifted IQ: Early Developmental Aspects*. New York: Plenum.

Gross, M.U.M. (1993) 'Nurturing the talents of exceptionally gifted individuals', in K.A. Heller, F.J. Monks & AH Passow, *International Handbook of Research and Development of Giftedness and Talent*. Oxford: Pergamon Press.

Grubar, J-C. (1985). 'Sleep and mental efficiency', in J. Freeman, (Ed.) *The Psychology of Gifted Children: Perspectives on Development and Education*. Chichester: Wiley.

Hansen, J.B. & Feldhusen, J.F. (1994), 'Comparison of trained and untrained teachers of gifted students' in *Gifted Child Quarterly, 38*, 115-121.

Hany, E. A. (1997) ' Modelling Teachers' Judgements of Giftedness: a Methodological Inquiry of Judgement Bias', *High Ability Studies, 8*, 159-178.

Hany, E.A. (1993), 'How teachers identify gifted students: feature processing or concept based classification', *European Journal for High Ability, 4*, 196-211.

Hany, E.A. (1995), 'Teachers' cognitive processes of identifying gifted students', in M.W. Katzko and F.J. Monks (Eds.) *Nurturing Talent; Individual Needs and Social Ability*. Assen, NL: Van Gorcum.

Hany, E.A. (1996). 'How leisure activities correspond to the development of creative achievement: insights from a study of highly intelligent individuals', *High Ability Studies, 7,* 65-82.

Heinbokel, A. (1997), 'Acceleration through grade-skipping in Germany'. *High Ability Studies, 861-77.*

Heller, K.A. & Hany, E.A. (1995), 'German-Chinese study on technical creativity: cross-cultural perspectives'. Paper presented at the World Council for Gifted and Talented Children meeting in Hong Kong.

Heller, K.A. & Ziegler, A. (1996/7) 'Gender differences in mathematics and natural sciences: can attributional retraining improve the low performance of gifted females?' *Gifted Child Quarterly, 41,* (In press)

Heller, K.A. (1995), 'Evaluation of programs for the gifted', in M.W. Katzko and F.J. Monks (Eds.) *Nurturing Talent; Individual Needs and Social Ability*. Assen, NL: Van Gorcum.

Heller, K.A., Osterrieder, K. Wystrychowski, (1995), 'A longitudinal follow-up evaluation study of a statewide acceleration program for highly gifted students at the German gymnasium', in M.W. Katzko and F.J. Monks (Eds.) *Nurturing Talent; Individual Needs and Social Ability*. Assen, NL: Van Gorcum.

Hess, R.D. & Azuma, H. (1991), 'Cultural support for schooling: Contrasts between Japan and the United States'. *Educ. Researcher, 20,* 2-9.

Heyman, G.D. & Dweck, C.S. (1996), 'Development of Motivation', in E. de Corte & F.E. Weinert (Eds.) *International Encyclopedia of Developmental and Instructional Psychology*. Oxford: Pergamon.

HMI (Her Majesty's Inspectorate) (1992). *The Education of Very Able Children in Maintained Schools. A review by HMI*. London: HMSO.

Holahan, C.K. & Sears, R.R. (1995). *The Gifted Group in Later Maturity*. Stanford, CA: Stanford University Press.

Jacobs, J.E. & Weisz, V. (1994), 'Gender stereotypes: implications for gifted education', *Roeper Review, 16,* 152-155.

Johnson, L.J. & Lewman, B.S. (1990), 'Parents' perceptions of the talents of young gifted boys and girls'. *Journal for the Education of the Gifted, 13,* 176-188.

Kanevsky, L. (1992), 'Gifted children and the learning process: insights on both from the research', in F. Monks and W. Peters (Eds.) *Talent for the Future*. Assen: Van Gorcum.

Kanevsky, L.S. (1994), 'A comparative study of children's learning in the zone of proximal development', *European Journal for High Ability, 5,* 163-175.

Kaufman, F.A. (1992). 'What educators can learn from gifted adults', in F.J. Monks & W. Peters (Eds.), *Talent for the Future,* Maastricht: Van Gorcum.

Kener, Y. (1993). 'Realistic and ideal self-concept of gifted children'. Unpublished MA thesis, Tel Aviv University (in Hebrew).

Kenny, D.A., Archambault, F. & Hallmark, B.W. (1995). *The Effects of Group Composition on Gifted and Non-gifted Elementary Students in Cooperative Learning Groups*. University of Connecticut, Research Monograph.

Kerry, T. & Kerry, C (1997). 'Teaching the more able; primary and secondary practice compared', *Education Today, 47,* 11-16.

Kolesaric, V. & Koren, I. (1992). 'The effect of identification and differential treatment of gifted elementary school pupils', *European Journal for High Ability, 3,* 155-163.

 Kulik, J.A. & Kulik, C. (1984). 'Synthesis of research on effects of accelerated instruction', *Educational Leadership,* October.

Lehwald, G. (1990). 'Curiosity and exploratory behaviour in ability development', *European Journal for High Ability, 1,* 204-210.

Luthar, S.S., Zigler, E. & Goldstein, D. (1992), 'Psychosocial adjustment among intellectually gifted adolescents: the role of cognitive-developmental and experiential factors', *Journal of Child Psychology and Psychiatry, 33,* 361-373.

Lykken, D.T., McGue, M., Tellegan, A. & Bouchard, T.J. (1992). 'Emergensis: genetic traits that may not run in families'. *American Psychologist, 47,* 1565-1577.

Maguin, E. & Loeber, R. (1996) 'Academic performance and delinquency', in Torry, M. & Morris, N. *Crime and Justice.* Chicago: Chicago University Press.

Maoz, N. (1993), 'Nurturing giftedness in non-school educative settings - using the personnel and material resources of the community', in K.A. Heller, F.J. Monks & A.H. Passow, *International Handbook of Research and Development of Giftedness and Talent.* Oxford: Pergamon Press.

Marsh, H.W., Chessor, D., Craven, R. & Roche, L. (1995), 'The effect of gifted and talented programs on academic self-concept: the big fish strikes again'. *American Educational Research Journal, 32,* 285-319.

Mascie-Taylor, C.G.N. (1989). 'Biological and social aspects of development', in N. Entwistle (Ed.) *Handbook of Educational Ideas and Practices,* London: Routledge.

Merenheimo, J. (1991), 'Cultural background and experience controlling the manifestation of giftedness'. *Scandinavian Journal of Educational Research, 2,* 115-129.

Milgram, R. M. & Hong, E (1997), 'Leisure activities and career development in intellectually gifted Israeli adolescents', in B. Bain, H. Janzen, J. Paterson, L. Stewin & A. Yu (Eds.) *Psychology and Education in the 21st Century.* Edmonton: ICP Press.

Milgram, R. M. (Ed.) (1991). *Counselling Gifted and Talented Children.* Norwood, NJ: Ablex Publishing.

Montgomery, D. (1996). *Educating the Able.* London: Cassell.

Moon, S.M., Feldhusen, J.F. & Dillon, D.R. (1994), 'Long-term effects of an enrichment program based on the Purdue Three-stage model', *Gifted Child Quarterly, 38,* 38-48.

MORI (1997) *Research Study Conducted for ISIS.* November-December 1996.

Nail, J.M. & Evans, J.G. (1997), 'The emotional adjustment of gifted adolescents: a view of global functioning'. Roeper Review, 20, 18-21.

NIAS (1994). *The Education of the More Able Child.* Northampton: NIAS.

Nisbet, J. (1990). 'Teaching thinking: an introduction to the research literature'. SCER *Spotlights, 26.*

OERI, 1993 (Office of Educational Research and Improvement, U.S. Department of Education). *National Excellence. A Case for Developing America's Talent.* Washington: US Department of Education.

Ojanen, S. & Freeman, J. (1994) *The Attitudes and Experiences of Headteachers, Class-Teachers, and Highly Able Pupils towards the Education of the Highly Able in Finland and Britain.* Savonlinna: University of Joensuu.

Oxfordshire (1995). *A Survey of Provision for More Able Pupils in 12 Oxford schools. Occasional Paper, No. 25.*

Palincsar, A. & Brown, A. (1984) 'Reciprocal teaching of comprehension - fostering and monitoring activities', *Cognition and Instruction,* 1, 117-75.

Paris, S.G. & Byrne, J.P. (1989). 'The Constructivist Approach to Self-regulation and Learning in the Classroom', in B.J. Zimmerman & D.H. Schunk (Eds.). *Self-regulated Learning and Academic Achievement: Theory, Research and Practice.* New York: Academic Press.

Passow, A.H. (1993), 'Educational programs for minority/disadvantaged students' in B. Wallace & H.B. Adams, *Worldwide Perspectives on the Gifted Disadvantaged. (Ed.)* Bicester: AB Academic Publishers.

Perleth, C. & Heller, K.A. (1994). 'The Munich longitudinal study of giftedness', in R.F. Subotnik, & K.D. Arnold, (Eds.) *Beyond Terman: contemporary longitudinal studies of giftedness and talent.* New Jersey: Ablex Publishing.

Perleth, C. (1993), 'Indicators of high ability in young children', in K.A. Heller, F.J. Monks & A.H. Passow, *International*

Handbook of Research and Development of Giftedness and Talent. Oxford: Pergamon Press.

Persson, R.S. (1998 in press), 'Paragons of virtue: teachers' conceptual understanding of high ability in an egalitarian school system', *High Ability Studies, 9.*

Peterson, J.S. & Margolin, K. (1997), 'Naming Gifted Children: An Example of Unintended "Reproduction", *Journal for the Education of the Gifted, 21,* 82-101.

Plomin, R., Owen, M.J. & McGuffin, P. (1994), 'The genetic basis of complex human behaviours', *Science, 264,* 1733-1739.

Prado, T.M. & Schiebel, W. (1995). 'Grade skipping: some German experiences'. *High Ability Studies, 6,* 60-72.

Radford, J. (1990). *Child Prodigies and Exceptional Early Achievers.* London: Harvester Wheatsheaf.

Renzulli, J.S. (1995). 'New directions for the schoolwide enrichment model', in M.W. Katzko and F.J. Monks (Eds.) *Nurturing Talent; Individual Needs and Social Ability.* Assen, NL: Van Gorcum.

Robinson, N. (1996), 'Counselling agendas for gifted young people: a commentary', *Journal for the Education of the Gifted, 20,* 128-137.

Robinson, W.P., Tayler, C.A. & Piolat, M. (1992), 'Redoublement in relation to self-perception and self-evaluation: France', *Research in Education, 47,* 64-75.

Rogers, K.B. & Span, P.(1993), 'Ability grouping with gifted and talented students: research and guidelines', in K.A. Heller, F.J. Monks, & A.H. Passow, *International Handbook of Research and Development of Giftedness and Talent.* Oxford: Pergamon.

Rost, D.H. & Czeschlik (1994), 'The psycho-social adjustment of gifted children in middle-childhood'. *European Journal of Psychology of Education, IX,* 15-25.

Rothman, G.R. (1992). 'Moral reasoning, moral behaviour, and moral giftedness: a developmental perspective', in Pnina S. Klein & A. J. Tannenbaum (Eds.) *To Be Young and Gifted.* New Jersey: Ablex.

Rowley, S. (1995), 'Identification and development of talent in young athletes', in J. Freeman, P. Span, & H. Wagner (Eds.). *Actualising Talent: a Lifelong Challenge.* London: Cassell.

Saunders, P. (1996). *Unequal but Fair? A Study of Class Barriers in Britain.* London: IEA Health and Welfare Unit.

Schaie, K.W. (1996). *Intellectual Development in Adulthood; The Seattle Longitudinal Study.* Cambridge: Cambridge University Press.

Shahal, N. (1995). 'Nurturing gifted children'. Paper presented at the World Council for Gifted and Talented Children meeting in Hong Kong.

Sharp, C., Hutchison, D., Davis, C. & Keys, W. (1996). *The Take-up of Advanced Science and Mathematics Courses: Summary Report.* London: School Curriculum and Assessment Authority

Sheblanova, H. (1966). 'A longitudinal study of intellectual and creative development in gifted primary school children', *High Ability Studies, 7,* 51-54.

Shore, B.M. & Delcourt, M.A.B. (1996), 'Effective curricular and program practices in gifted education and the interface with general education', *Journal for the Education of the Gifted, 20,* 138-154..

Shore, B.M. & Kanevsky, L.S. (1993), 'Thinking processes: being and becoming gifted', in Heller, K.A., Monks, F.J. &. Passow, H.A. (Eds.) (1993) *International Handbook of Research and Development of Giftedness and Talent.* Oxford: Pergamon Press.

Shore, B.M., Coleman, E.B. & Moss, E. (1992), 'Cognitive psychology and the use of protocols in the understanding of giftedness and high level thinking', in F. Monks and W. Peters (Eds.) *Talent for the Future.* Assen: Van Gorcum.

Shore, B.M., Cornell, D.G., Robinson, A. & Ward, V.S. (1991). *Recommended Practices in Gifted Education: A Critical Analysis.* N.Y: Teachers College Press.

Silverman, L.K. (1993), 'The gifted individual' in L.K. Silverman (Ed.) *Counselling the Gifted and Talented.* Denver: Love.

Simonton, D.K. (1988). *Scientific Genius. A Psychology of Science.* Cambridge: Cambridge University Press.

Simonton, D.K. (1994), 'Emergence and realization of genius; the lives and works of 120 classical composers'. *Journal of Personality and Social Psychology, 61,* 829-840.

Simonton, D.K. (1994). *Greatness: Who Makes History and Why.* New York: The Guildford Press.

Sloboda, J. (1993), 'Musical ability', in Bock, G.R. & Ackrill, K.A. *The Origins and Development of High Ability* (Ciba Foundation Symposium) Chichester: Wiley.

Sloboda, J., Davidson, J.W., Howe, M.J.A. & Moore, D.G. (1996), 'The role of practice in the development of performing musicians', *British Journal of Psychology, 87,* 287-309.

Smithers, A. (1997). 'The supply of, and demand for, scientists and engineers', SBS lecture, Association for Science Education, Birmingham, 2 January.

Southern, W.T. & Jones, E.D. (Eds.) (1991) *The Academic Acceleration of Gifted Children*. New York: Teachers College Press.

Southern, W.T., Jones, E.D. & Stanley, J.C. (1993), 'Acceleration and enrichment: the content and development of program options', in Heller, K.A., Monks, F.J. &. Passow, H.A. (Eds.) *International Handbook of Research and Development of Giftedness and Talent*. Oxford: Pergamon Press.

Span, P. (1995). 'Self-regulated learning by highly able children', in J. Freeman, P. Span, & H. Wagner (Eds.) *Actualising Talent: a Lifelong Challenge*. London: Cassell.

Stanley, J.C. (1990) 'Finding and Helping Young People with Exceptional Mathematical Reasoning Ability', in: Howe M.J.A. (Ed.) *Encouraging the Development of Exceptional Skills and Talents*. Leicester: BPS pp211-221

Stanley, J.C.(1993) quoted in Bock, G.R. & Ackrill, K.A. *The Origins and Development of High Ability* (Ciba Foundation Symposium) Chichester: Wiley.

Stapf, A. (1990). 'Hochbegabte Mädchen: Entwicklung, Identifikation und Beratung, insbesondere im Vorschualter (Highly able girls: development, identification and counselling, especially at pre-school age)'. In *Hochbegabte Mädchen,* W. Wieczerkowski & T.M. Prado (Eds.). Bad Honnef: K. H. Bock.

Stedtnitz, U. (1995) 'Psychosocial dimensions of high ability: a review of major issues and neglected topics' in J. Freeman, P. Span, & H. Wagner (Eds.) *Actualizing Talent: a Lifelong Challenge*. London: Cassell.

Sternberg, R, & Grigorenko, E. (1997). *Intelligence, Heredity and Environment.* Cambridge: Cambridge University Press.

Sternberg, R. J. (1985). *Beyond IQ: a Triarchic Theory of Human Intelligence.* Cambridge: Cambridge University Press.

Sternberg, R.J. & Lubart, T.I. (1995). *Defying the Crowd; Cultivating Creativity in a Culture of Conformity.* New York: Free Press.

Sternberg, R.J. (1997), 'Educating intelligence: infusing the Triarchic Theory into school instruction', in *Intelligence, Heredity and Environment*, R.J. Sternberg & E.Grigorenko (Eds.) Cambridge: Cambridge University Press.

Sternberg, R.J.(1993), 'Procedures for identifying intellectual potential in the gifted: a perspective on alternative 'metaphors of mind', in K.A. Heller, F.J. Monks & A.H. Passow, *International Handbook of Research and Development of Giftedness and Talent*. Oxford: Pergamon Press.

Subotnik, R., Kassan, L., Summers, E. & Wasser, A. (1993). *Genius Revisited: High IQ Children Grow Up*. New Jersey: Ablex.

Swiatek, M.A. & Benbow, C.P. (1991) 'Ten-year longitudinal follow-up of ability-matched accelerated and unaccelerated gifted students'. *Journal of Educational Psychology, 4,* 528-538.

Sylva, K. (1994). 'School influences on children's development', *J. Child Psychol. Psychiat., 35,* 135-170

Tempest, N.R. (1974) *Teaching Clever Children 7-11*. London: Routledge and Kegan Paul.

Terassier, J-C, (1985). 'Dysynchrony: uneven development', in J. Freeman (Ed.) *The Psychology of Gifted Children*. Chichester: John Wiley.

Terman, L.M. (1925-1929). *Genetic Studies of Genius* Vols. I-V, Stanford: Stanford University Press.

TES (Times Educational Supplement) (1997). Secretary for State for Education reported on page 13, January 10.

Torrance, E.P. (1987), 'Teaching for creativity' in S.G. Isaksen (Ed.) *Frontiers of Creativity Research*. Buffalo, New York: Bearly.

Treffinger, D.J. & Feldhusen, J.F. (1996), 'Talent recognition and development: successor to gifted education'. *Journal for the Education of the Gifted, 19,* 181-193.

Trost, G. (1993), 'Prediction of excellence in school, university and work', in K.A. Heller, F.J. Monks & A.H. Passow, *International Handbook of Research and Development of Giftedness and Talent*. Oxford: Pergamon Press.

Turner, G. (1996), 'Intelligence and the X chromosome', *Lancet, 347,* 1814-15.

UFA (University of the First Age) (1996) *Pilot Phase One: Report on Summer School 1996*. Birmingham Education Dept.

Urban, K.K. (1995), 'Different models in describing, exploring, explaining and nurturing creativity in society', *European Journal for High Ability, 6,* 143-159.

van Leishout, C.F.M. (1995) 'Development of social giftedness and gifted personality in context' in M.W. Katzko and F.J. Monks (Eds.) *Nurturing Talent; Individual Needs and Social Ability*. Assen, NL: Van Gorcum.

Wagner, H. (1995) 'Non-school provision for talent development', in J. Freeman, P. Span, & H. Wagner (Eds.) *Actualising Talent: a Lifelong Challenge*. London: Cassell.

Wagner, H., Neber, H. & Heller, K.A. (1995) 'The BundesSchülerAkademie: a residential summer program for gifted adolescents in Germany', in M.W. Katzko and F.J. Monks (Eds.) *Nurturing Talent; Individual Needs and Social Ability*. Assen, NL: Van Gorcum.

Walberg, H.J. (1995), 'Nurturing children for adult success', in M.W. Katzko and F.J. Monks (Eds.) *Nurturing Talent; Individual Needs and Social Ability*. Assen, NL: Van Gorcum.

Wallace, B. & Adams H.B. (Eds.) (1993). *Worldwide Perspectives on the Gifted Disadvantaged*. Bicester: AB Academic Publishers.

Webb, J.T. (1993), 'Nurturing social-emotional development of gifted children', in K.A. Heller, F.J. Monks & A.H. Passow, *International Handbook of Research and Development of Giftedness and Talent*. Oxford: Pergamon Press.

Weisberg, R. (1992). *Creativity, Genius and Other Myths*. New York: Freeman.

Wertsch, J. D. (1990). *Voices of the Mind: a Sociocultural Approach to Mediated Action*. London: Harvester Wheatsheaf.

West, A. & West, R. (1997), 'Examination results of pupils offered Assisted Places: comparing GCE Advanced level results in independent and state schools', *Educational Studies, 23,* 287-293.

West, T. (1991). *In the Mind's Eye.* Buffalo: Prometheus.

White, K.R. (1992), 'The relation between socio-economic status and academic achievement'. *Psychological Bulletin, 91,* 461-481.

Winner, E. (1996). *Gifted Children: Myths and Realities.* New York: Basic Books.

Wood, D., Wood, H., Ainsworth, S. & O'Malley, C. (1995), 'On becoming a tutor: toward an ontogenetic model'. *Cognition and Instruction, 13 (4),* 565-581.

Yewchuk, C. & Jobagy, S. (1991). 'Gifted adolescents: at risk for suicide', *European Journal for High Ability, 2,* 73-85.

Zha, Z. (1995a). 'Development of research and education of gifted children in China'. Paper given in Beijing, China, August.

Zha, Z. (1995b), 'The influence of family education on gifted children'. Paper presented at World Conference on Gifted and Talented Children, Hong Kong.

Zorman, R. (1996). 'The long and winding road from promise to fulfilment in science among gifted females in Israel', *High Ability Studies, 7,* 39-50.

Zorman, R. (1997). 'Eureka: the cross-cultural model for identification of hidden talent through enrichment', *Roeper Review, 20,* 54-61.

Zukerman, H. (1977). *Scientific Elite: Nobel Laureates in the United States.* New York: Free Press.

Printed in the UK for The Stationery Office
J44845, C25, 4/98, 5673